TRAPUNTO
by Machine

Hari Walner

C&T PUBLISHING

Trapunto by Machine ©1996 Hari Walner

EDITORS: Louise Townsend and Liz Aneloski
COPY EDITOR: Judith M. Moretz
TECHNICAL EDITOR: Diana Roberts

FRONT COVER DESIGN: Suzanne Staud
BACK COVER AND BOOK DESIGN: Irene Morris
ILLUSTRATIONS: Hari Walner

QUILT PHOTOGRAPHS: Brian Birlauf, Denver, Colorado

AUTHOR PHOTOGRAPH: Pat Santaniello
QUILTERS' PHOTOGRAPHS: Courtesy of the quilters
STUDIO PHOTOGRAPHS: Hari Walner and Gordon Snow

Published by C&T Publishing, Inc., P.O. Box 1456, Lafayette, California 94549

ISBN: 1-57120-006-1

Library of Congress Cataloging-in-Publication Data

Walner, Hari, 1940—
      Trapunto by machine / Hari Walner
         p.   .ca
      Includes bibliographical references.
      ISBN 1-57120-006-1
      1. Trapunto—Patterns. 2. Machine quilting—Patterns. I. Title
      TTB35.W3554 1996
      746.46—dc20   95-49956
                                                    CIP

Simplicity's Bond Tight is a brand name of Air Lite Synthetics Manufacturing.

Poly-fil® Cotton Classic®, Hi-Loft®, Ultra-Loft®, and Extra-Loft® are registered trademarks of
   Fairfield Processing Corp.
Heirloom® Cotton Batting is a registered trademark of Hobbs Bonded Fibers.
Fatt Batt and Cotton Choice are brand names of Mountain Mist®. Mountain Mist® is a registered trademark
   of Stearns Technical Textiles Company.
Warm and Natural is a trademark of Warm Products, Inc.
Fiskars for Kids™ is a trademark of Fiskars Inc.
Wash Away™ is distributed by YLI

Printed in Hong Kong
10 9 8 7 6

Table of Contents

Dedication

In Memory of Louise Owens Townsend
(1942-1995)

The dedication of this book is a thank you to Louise O. Townsend for her devotion to the world of quilts and her friendship to quilters. All quilters have in some way benefited, or will benefit, from Louise's commitment to our art. She set and maintained high standards while serving as Managing Editor of *Quilter's Newsletter Magazine* for many years. She participated enthusiastically with the American Quilt Study Group documenting our quilt heritage. She gave personal input and encouragement to quilters from everywhere, and of every skill level.

This quilter in particular owes an unpayable debt of gratitude to Louise, for her gentle confidence in me when I first began blending my life with quilts in 1987. In the years since, she showed unbelievably good humor and patience whenever I was foot-dragging about publishing designs, ideas, and techniques.

More recently, as book editor at C&T Publishing, she nudged me to do this book. Louise knew well, and practiced, the art of applied friendship. I have greatly benefited from this practice.

To Louise O. Townsend from all of us, thank you. To Louise from me, love and thank you.
—*Hari Walner*

Thank You

To Gordon Snow, my partner in life and business, for the meaningful efforts and understanding he has given throughout this project.

To Ned and Kim Harding of Boulder, Colorado for their time and expertise helping my PC programs communicate with C&T's MAC system.

To Lynn Shufflebein, from Sioux Falls, South Dakota, for sharing her knowledge of computer programs.

To Viking of America and the Pfaff Corporation for the use of their terrific sewing machines.

To the folks at C&T, for their confidence in this book. A special thank you to Liz Aneloski, my editor, for doing a graceful and excellent job of stepping in and filling some very big editorial shoes.

The Ties That Bind

Cheryl Osborn and Ramona Hilton helped in every way imaginable while I stumbled through the maze... Thank you to these dear friends that I have known since junior high school.

Preface

This book will show you how to do trapunto quilting by machine without having to make little openings in the back of your quilt. It will also explain how to develop your own stippling technique, and other stitching ideas that will complement your trapunto work.

In our quilt world, the word trapunto refers to the techniques that raise elements of a quilting design. Although the task of stuffing is time consuming, these techniques give the effect of bas-relief sculpture that we often see on the walls and facades of buildings. Traditionally this has been done by making tiny holes in the back of the quilt, stuffing the various motifs with additional batting or yarn and then closing the holes. These raised motifs add textural richness to a finished quilt. This new technique will give you these same beautiful results much more easily.

Because the lessons in this book call for free-motion quilting, the first part of this book is a review of basic machine quilting tools and techniques, with an emphasis on free-motion quilting. There are many excellent books available that go into more detail about many other aspects of machine quilting. (See bibliography.)

The second part contains six lessons, each lesson introducing another way to add texture to your quilt. Quilts made by incorporating one or more of these techniques and designs are shown throughout the book. (The quiltmakers are shown at the back of the book.)

The next part of the book contains more original quilting designs, complete with directions. These patterns were designed to be used with several, if not all, of the techniques. You, being the creative soul that you are, will take many of these simple techniques and designs to much greater heights. My happy thoughts are with you.

About the piecing instructions in this book...

There aren't any.

This book is about quilting techniques. The quilts shown in this book are examples of how quilters have used these techniques and designs in their work. Many excellent books about piecing, appliqué, finishing and binding are available. Ask your quilt shop or bookseller.

The Sharing Spirit of Quilting

The basic trapunto technique (Lesson 2) converged from a variety of inspirations and sources.

A couple of years ago I began to see water-soluble basting thread for sale. I bought a spool here and there, even though I didn't have a clue as to how I would use it in my work. Water-soluble thread just seemed like a clever idea for something.

Then I read an article on layered trapunto by Lois Morrison in *Quilts and Quilting* (©1991 Taunton Press, Inc.) that inspired me to begin seriously thinking about how I might trapunto my quilts. At a workshop with Cheryl Phillips, Cheryl shared how she added a first layer of batting without a quilt backing to get a trapunto effect. Great idea.

Judy Morin wrote an article about a similar trapunto technique, using nylon monofilament and then stitching back over it, in order to better define the motifs. Judy's article made me think about using a different thread for the initial stitching.

The next time I glanced at those packages of water-soluble thread, they said, "Use me, use me." I did and it worked. What fun.

My sincere thanks and appreciation to these generous quilter-artist-teacher-innovators who have shared their work and their techniques. Cheryl and Judy have each made a quilt for this book. Their quilts are shown in the quilt gallery.

A detail from Let's Play *by Margie Evans*

First Things First
Machine Quilting Basics

For those who haven't yet tried machine quilting, this first section is designed to give a very basic understanding of tools and techniques for machine quilting in general, and free-motion quilting in particular.

If you already quilt with your sewing machine but still have a few questions, or need a little help with some aspects of your machine quilting, a quick run through this section might yield a hint or two that will help you. If you are already familiar with all facets of machine quilting, and are comfortable with your skill level, you might want to skip this part and go right to the lessons on trapunto and texture beginning on page 26.

Tools and Accessories

Sewing Machines

You do not need a new, top-of-the-line sewing machine, even though we would all like to have one (one of each, please). You do need a clean sewing machine in good working order and the accessories that will eliminate frustration.

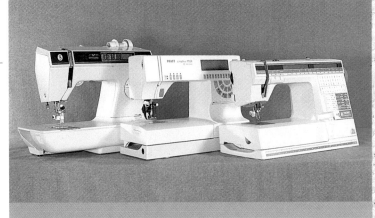

Speed: For free-motion quilting techniques, experience shows that an electronic pedal does not heat up like the older electric pedals do. Machines that only run "very fast" or "stop" are difficult to use for machine quilting. It is very helpful to be able to control the speed of your machine.

Accessories: Helpful accessories are usually easy to find, and most sewing machine manufacturers make the basic accessories that you need to quilt with your machine. Some are included as standard equipment with the machine when it is purchased. If the manufacturer of your machine does not make an accessory you need, you can often find a generic accessory or one made by another sewing machine manufacturer that will fit your machine.

Cleaning: Your owner's manual can give you tips on how to clean and, if necessary, oil your machine. If your manual fails to help, ask your dealer for suggestions. She will gladly share advice on the best care for your machine. You will never regret learning how to clean and maintain your machine in good working order.

There is a wide variety of sewing machines, each with its own specialties and eccentricities. The better you know and understand your machine, the happier you will be with it. Think of it as your partner in art. The one rule that applies to all machines? Cleanliness.

Walking Foot

For straight-line quilting a walking foot (also called an even-feed foot) is worth the investment. This foot has a different feel to it than a regular presser foot and at first may feel a bit cumbersome; but give it a fair trial and you will see the benefits of using this foot. Some models of the Pfaff sewing machine have a built-on even-feed foot.

The movement of a walking foot. A walking foot's unique trait is that it has feed dogs that move in rhythm with the needle, which moves in rhythm with the lower feed dogs. This simultaneous movement of upper and lower feed dogs helps to move all layers of the quilt through the sewing machine at the same pace. The basic technique pages will show you when to use this foot.

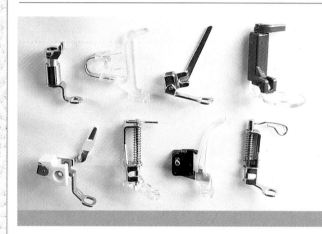

Darning Foot

A good darning foot is extremely helpful when you are free-motion quilting, and there is a wide variety available. Other names for this type of foot are free-embroidery foot and quilting foot. What makes this foot so desirable is that it allows you the freedom to move your fabric side to side and front to back.

The movement of a darning foot. The foot moves up and down with the needle. The foot is down and holds the fabric when the needle is in the fabric. When the needle moves up and out of the fabric, the foot lifts too, freeing your fabric so you can move it. Then, just before the needle re-enters the fabric, the foot moves down again and holds the fabric down so the needle can make a good stitch.

The freedom to move your fabric side to side, back to front, and front to back at will is necessary in free-motion quilting, and a foot that holds the fabric while a stitch is being made helps avoid skipped stitches.

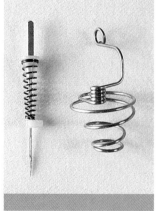

Can't find a darning foot to fit your machine? One alternative to a darning foot is a spring needle. This is a sewing machine needle set into a small spring with a small plastic gasket at the end of the spring to help steady the fabric when the needle makes the stitch. You can replace the needle when it gets dull.

Another possibility is to use a spring attachment. You often have to bend or manipulate this spring to fit your particular machine. If you glue a rubber washer to the end of the spring, it helps hold the fabric steady while stitching. Some machine quilters stitch with an open needle (no foot). If you decide to try this, please be very careful with the placement of your fingers.

Thread

Select thread you enjoy using that also gives the look you want for your quilt.

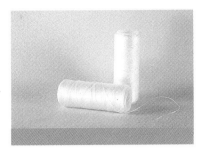

Many techniques in this book use water-soluble basting thread. This thread is used for basting and dissolves quickly in water. It is very useful for the machine trapunto technique.

For machine quilting, 100% cotton machine embroidery thread, 50 weight, is terrific. Exotic threads, rayons, silks, metallics and iridescent blends are also fun and useful in achieving special effects.

Many quilts have been stitched with fine (.004) nylon monofilament thread. I don't care for the way the spun nylon reflects the light, but you should try a variety of threads to find out what you do and do not like. Nobody can do your art better than you.

Needles

Match the type of needle to the thread you have chosen. A jeans/denim needle, size 70, is a good match with 50 weight machine embroidery thread for many sewing machines, but you must experiment to find what works best for you. The jeans/denim needle has a very sharp stiletto point and penetrates the layers of a quilt with authority.

A clean, sharp needle is a must.
Change your needle often.

When using water-soluble basting thread, a machine embroidery needle, size 75, works well. These embroidery needles are made to prevent excessive fraying when stitching with tempermental threads. Because of this, machine embroidery needles are also good to use with the exotic threads.

Fabric

The techniques in this book work well with 100% cotton fabric, the choice of most quilters, although it is not a necessity. Regardless of the fabric type and fiber content you prefer, always use good quality fabric. Many beautiful quilts have been made with wool, silk, linen, polyester, and cotton-polyester blends.

Fabrics that differ in fiber content often iron and crease at different temperatures. An iron hot enough to press cotton well will often cause another fiber to pucker. This can be a problem when seaming different types of fabric together. The cleaning process also varies from fabric to fabric, so if you want to use some fabrics that must be dry-cleaned, make sure the other fabrics in your quilt project can also be dry-cleaned.

Use only the tools and materials that work best for your quilt art. Although most of us use the same common words, through careful selection and arrangement, none of us write the same poems.

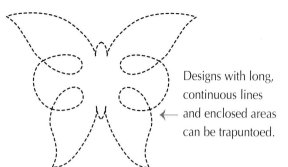

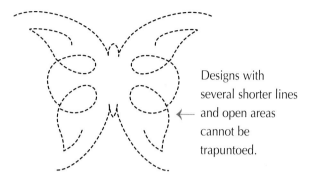

The Next Steps

Choosing a Quilting Pattern for the Methods in this Book

Designs with long, continuous lines and enclosed areas can be trapuntoed.

Designs with several shorter lines and open areas cannot be trapuntoed.

Choose patterns designed with long continuous lines so you won't have to start and stop often. These designs are easier to quilt and your overall quilting will be much smoother.

Because the techniques in the lesson section of this book add texture to quilting designs, these techniques call for designs whose motifs and elements are enclosed, as opposed to being open. All the designs in this book are appropriate for these techniques in particular and for machine quilting in general.

Marking Suggestions

Clear marking of your quilting design is very important in machine quilting because you need to see your lines as you stitch, without having to stop and study them.

Straight line quilting. For straight-line quilting you can use tape as a guide. Do not leave tape on your quilt overnight, and do not expose it to heat. The adhesive might transfer to your fabric. Stitch alongside the tape, not through it. There are also guides that you can attach to your walking foot that help keep lines parallel. Ask your dealer which ones will work for your machine.

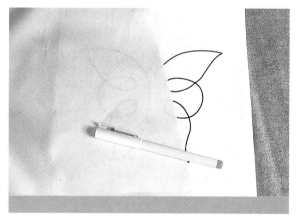

Free-motion quilting. For free-motion quilting, mark your quilt top so you can see the marks easily as you stitch. On light, solid fabrics you can often see the design through the fabric, making it easier to trace it with your favorite marker. On darker fabrics, use a light box and a light opaque pencil.

Stencils are especially useful after you have put a quilt sandwich together and can no longer see through the fabric. You can buy lovely stencils with machine quilting designs or buy soft stencil plastic and cut your own with a double-bladed craft knife.

Marking is difficult when you need to see the lines on a heavily patterned fabric. One-color markers won't do, and using several colors is time consuming and confusing. Try this idea:

1 Stack eight to ten sheets of thin, crisp artists' tracing paper. Mark the quilting design on one sheet only. Pin the sheets together with the marked sheet on top.

2 Remove the thread from your sewing machine and insert a large, dull needle. Stitch through the stack of paper as though you were free-motion quilting and perforate the entire design. This will make stitchable, disposable stencils.

3 When you are ready to stitch that design, pin one of the perforated design sheets to your quilt sandwich and stitch through the paper on the design lines. Because the design lines on the paper are perforated twice (once when you made the throw-away stencil with the threadless machine and once when you quilted through it), the paper stencil tears away easily.

Choosing Batting

Combine the techniques in this book with different types of batting to achieve a variety of effects. In each lesson there is a suggestion as to what batt(s) could be used for that technique, but these are only suggestions. There is no perfect batting for every use that will suit everyone's tastes, but there are some basic batting traits to consider. For detailed information about batting, check the bibliography and sources under batting.

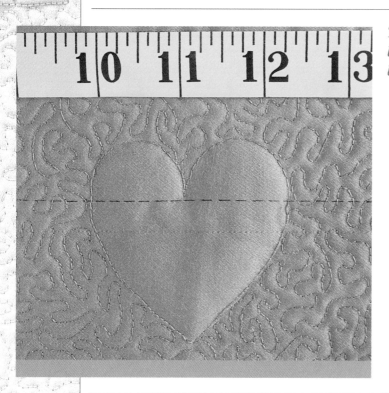

The cross sections of batts shown below were quilted as shown here before being cut.

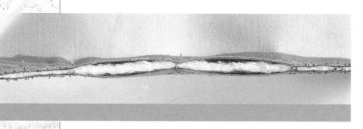

Cotton and cotton-blend batts cling to fabric and are by far the easiest to machine quilt. Cotton batts have a low loft (they are not fluffy), they drape well and have a softer look. Most cotton batts come prepackaged in standard sizes.

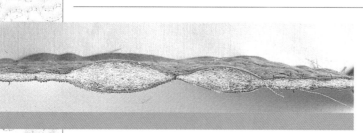

Polyester batts and wool batts tend to shift more in the quilt sandwich and need to be basted more securely for machine quilting. Because polyester and wool batts have a higher loft than cotton batts, you can achieve puffy effects with them that you cannot achieve with a cotton batt.

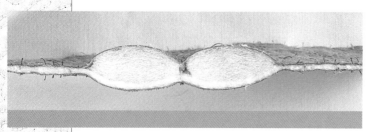

Try using a variety of batts. Since companies have different methods of manufacturing, batts made of the same fibers can differ a great deal. You can use extra thick polyester batt in the design area, layered with cotton batt for machine trapunto.

Basting

Baste very securely with safety pins or one of the new tacking guns for machine quilting. Be sure to eliminate wrinkles and puckers from your backing, batting, and quilt top.

Supporting Your Quilt

When machine quilting, you need to be able to manipulate your quilt freely, smoothly, and unencumbered at all times. Your quilt must be well supported and free of stress. It is very difficult to stitch when your quilt is hanging off the edge of a table or your sewing machine. The slightest weight of the quilt will tug at the needle and cause uneven stitches and frustration.

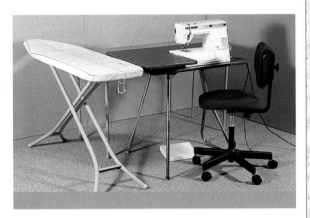

Construct support wherever your quilt needs it. If your machine sits on a table, build up the area around your machine or purchase a portable extension table for your machine. If your machine is in a cabinet, put a card table at the back and on the left. You can also lower your ironing board to the height of your sewing table for support.

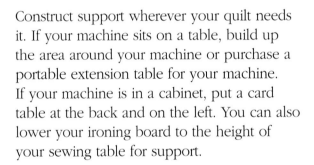

Controlling Your Quilt

There is not much room on the sewing machine bed. Gather the part of the quilt that will be in the machine in large, soft folds. Use large office binder clips or quilter's clips to prevent these folds from coming undone. I don't like to roll a quilt because the roll takes on the personality of a telephone pole. This stiff pole, although neat and tidy, is difficult to manipulate. Use the back of a chair to hold the part of the quilt that is on the bed and in front of the machine.

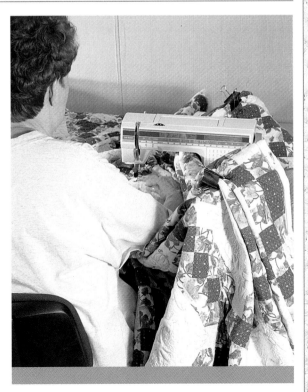

■ **Be sure to mark the edges of your batt when you first cut it into thirds so you can match the correct edges when putting the sections back together.**

■ **When quilting the middle third, you do not need to quilt the borders. When quilting borders, most of the quilt is outside the machine bed anyway.**

■ **Loosely pin the side sections of the quilt top and backing together when you are quilting the middle section. This will prevent them from separating and possibly becoming distorted.**

Quilting

Quilting a Large Quilt

To eliminate much of the bulk of a large quilt in the machine, try this method of basting.

I first read this idea in Debra Wagner's book, *Teach Yourself Machine Piecing and Quilting.* Thanks from me and many other quilters.

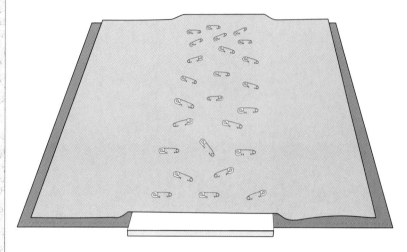

1 Cut your lining and batting to size. Cut the batting into thirds lengthwise and layer the middle third only with the complete backing and quilt top. Pin baste this middle section of the quilt sandwich securely and quilt to within 2"-3" of the edge of the batting.

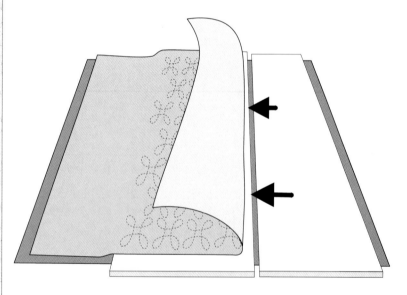

2 When the middle third has been quilted, peel back the quilt top and butt one of the side thirds of the batt up against the middle, being careful to match the edges. Do not overlap the edges. Loosely hand baste these batt sections together.

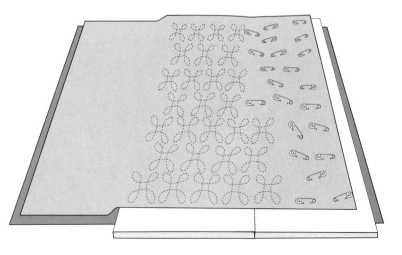

3 Pin baste this third of the quilt sandwich. After it is quilted, turn your quilt around and add the last third of the batting. Baste and quilt the last section.

Moving the Quilt in the Sewing Machine

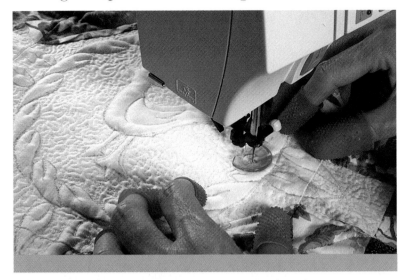

You must be able to move your quilt freely. Gripping or holding the quilt tightly will result in sore fingers, arms, shoulders, and neck. You will be a very tired puppy at the end of a quilting session.

Make a quilt nest around the area you are stitching and be sure the area inside that nest is completely free of stress.

TIPS

■ **Check again to be sure the quilt is completely free to move.** If it is falling off the edge of your machine, cabinet or table, the slightest tug will pull the stitches out of the "ditch".

■ **"See" what you are stitching.** I am not joking or making "light" of this problem. Use extra lighting if necessary.

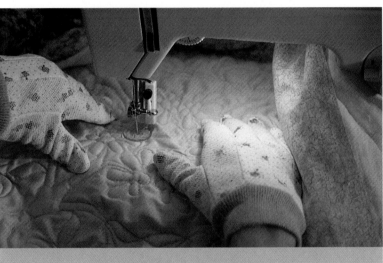

Wear something on your fingers or hands that will give you traction and allow you to guide your quilt instead of gripping it. I use loosely fitting rubber office fingers that have rubber bumps on them. These give me the best traction without making my hands hot. Other quilters use garden gloves with bumps on them, rubber gloves, or the cut-off finger tips from rubber gloves.

Straight-Line Quilting

Although we are attracted to beautiful, graceful quilting motifs, straight-line quilting serves important purposes. One purpose is to stabilize a quilt by stitching directly next to seam lines, called stitching-in-the-ditch. It can also be an important complement to other design work, the most obvious example being when grid quilting is used in the background of a very graceful design. The feed dogs on your machine should be engaged for straight-line quilting. If possible, use a walking or even-feed foot.

TIPS

■ **Keep your eye on the straight line you want to stitch. Do not watch the needle. The needle is only moving up and down. Your quilt is doing all the moving (toward the needle), so that is what you need to watch and control. Watching the line ⅛" to ¼" in front of the needle is usually enough to help you guide your quilt into the needle.**

To Begin

1 Place your quilt in your machine at the position you wish to start quilting. Pull the bobbin thread to the top. Hold the top thread and turn the hand wheel toward you until the needle makes one complete cycle. This will pull a loop of the bobbin thread to the top. Pull this loop until the end of the bobbin thread is on the top of your quilt. This will prevent threads from tangling underneath your quilt.

2 To secure (knot) your stitches, set your stitch length right next to but not at 0. Hold the ends of both threads (top and bobbin) and take five or six stitches. These tiny stitches will not pull out.

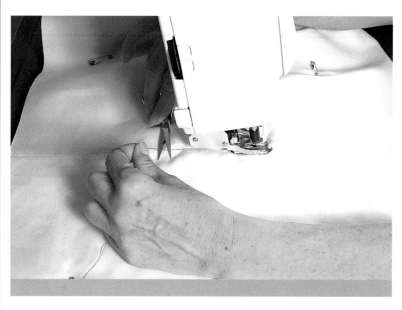

3 Return your stitch length to your desired size and begin quilting. After you stitch for a couple of inches, cut off the tails of the threads. An alternative is to thread these threads through a needle and bury them in the batt.

4 Let the quilt sandwich feed easily up to the needle, with absolutely no tension on the fabric. Keep the sandwich in front of the needle relaxed and slightly "scrunched." It can also be helpful to keep one hand on each side of the needle to keep the fabric flattened and smooth.

5 When you finish a line of stitching, again set your stitch length to "tiny" and secure (knot) your threads.

Free-Motion Quilting

It is free-motion quilting skills that give machine quilters that wonderful feeling of freedom and creativity. Free-motion quilting is using your machine to quilt curves and graceful designs with very little turning of the quilt sandwich.

Moving around freely. For free-motion quilting, lower or cover your feed dogs and attach a darning foot. Feed dogs control the length of the stitches and the direction of the fabric. In free-motion quilting we do not let the feed dogs have this control. Feed dogs have no way of knowing what quilting design lines they should follow, so even if you have one of those terrific machines with multi-directional stitching, you still need to disengage your feed dogs so you can move the fabric freely.

Use skills you already have. The skills needed to free-motion quilt are simple and are ones that you already possess. Maybe you haven't put them all together before. The simple continuous-line quilting design on page 21 is good to practice with. You only need to move fabric in any direction and control your machine's speed.

You Can

1 Move fabric in your sewing machine in any direction.

Exercise

Mark a quilting design on a scrap of plain fabric (10"-14"). Be sure the feed dogs are disengaged and your darning foot is attached. Do not run the motor, just move the fabric around under the needle. Move it side to side, back to front, front to back, following the line of the design. That is how you will be moving the quilt when you are quilting. Now you know you can move the fabric in any direction. **Hold that thought.**

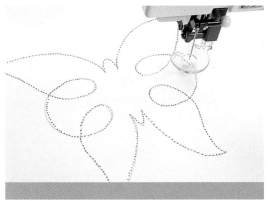

2 Control the power given to your sewing machine.

Exercise

Mark a quilting design on a piece of plain paper. Take the thread out of your needle and put in an old, dull needle. Put the paper under the needle, lower the presser foot, give the machine power, and "stitch" the design on the paper. The distance between the holes in the paper would be the length of the stitches. Experiment with running the machine at different speeds.

If you move the paper at a constant speed you will see that the faster your machine runs, the smaller the stitches. When you slow your machine down, the stitches get longer. This shows that you can control the speed of your machine while moving your project. It is the combination of how fast you move your fabric and how much speed you give your machine that determines the evenness of your machine stitches. With practice, you will decide the combination that works best for you.

When you first begin to free-motion quilt, you tend to think you are out of control, but the opposite is true. Now you really are in control. (Scary, isn't it?) Your sewing machine is not going to help guide your fabric or determine the stitch length. Take advantage of this control and have a good time.

To Begin

Pull the bobbin thread through to the top. (See Straight-line Quilting.)

1 To lock your threads, hold the top and bobbin thread out of the way and make several tiny stitches right next to each other. *You need to move your quilt slightly* in order to do this. The feed dogs will not advance the fabric. Try to make these stitches right next to each other instead of on top of each other. Making the stitches right on top of each other results in a little nub on the back of your quilt. Begin and finish lines of quilting this way.

2 Begin moving your fabric toward the needle, keeping your eye on the line of the design right in front of the needle. After you have stitched a few inches, stop and cut off the threads very close to the fabric. An alternative is to thread these threads through a needle and bury them in the batt.

Gently guide your fabric front to back, back to front, and side to side, watching the line of your design and feeding it into the needle. Work at moving your fabric at a steady pace and keeping your machine at a steady speed.

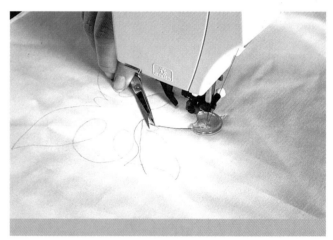

3 When you need to move from one line to another, secure the stitches on the line you are stitching. Lift your presser foot lever to release the upper thread tension and slide your fabric to where you want to begin the next line. Lower the presser foot lever and secure the new line of stitches. Later on you can clip the connecting threads (top and bobbin).

Speed

The speed you free-motion quilt should be considered. Some quilters find if they stitch fast and move the fabric at a good pace, they avoid the uneven stitches that occur from hesitating. I have tried this and it is true, but I much prefer to stitch at a medium-slow speed because I find it more relaxing. I maintain an even pace and follow my design because I am not as tense as when I try to stitch fast. Some of us are sprinters, some of us are milers. You should experiment with stitching fast and slow, and find the speed you are most comfortable with.

···Helpful Hints···

■ Avoid stopping your stitching while on a curve. In the beginning it is difficult to catch the flow of the curve when you start up again.

■ Stop stitching where lines intersect, or at a point.

■ When your design has a sharp point in it, take an extra stitch at that point to avoid rounding it off.

■ While in the midst of free-motion stitching, if you find that you need to stitch a straighter line for a short time, try raising your feed dogs temporarily. You will still need to guide your fabric with the darning foot, but the feed dogs below the fabric will help a little.

TIPS

■ **Don't forget to breathe. You need oxygen. Relax and have fun. No one ever died from a drive-by quilting.**

When the Cat Jumps on Your Quilt While You Are Quilting . . .or, How to Survive a Free-Motion Mistake Without Grief

Learning to relax while machine quilting is easier when you know how to recover quickly from a mistake. No matter the cause, sometimes we just goof. When that happens:

1 Recognize that it is not what you want. Stop stitching immediately and raise your presser foot to release the thread tension. Do not secure (lock) your stitches.

2 Slide your quilt back to where you were several stitches *before* you drifted from the line. Lower the presser foot right on top of the previous "good stitches" and secure your thread as usual.

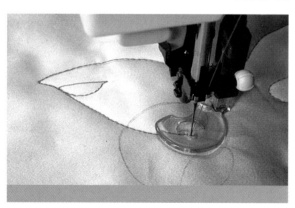

3 Continue stitching your design. By starting your corrected line on top of stitches that were made before you drifted, you will secure the stitches of the old and new lines at the same time.

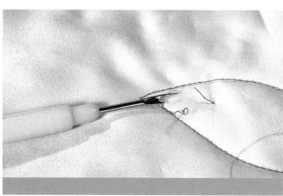

4 When convenient, just take your handy little seam ripper and remove the errant stitches.

Is It a Mistake or an Interpretation?

Keep in mind that even if you do drift off a line, the drawn line of the design will be washed off. If your newly stitched line is still graceful and in keeping with the idea that you have in mind, it is not a mistake, it is an adaptation. Maybe your own unconscious sense of grace and beauty is at work here.

SOLO FLIGHT Ready to free-motion quilt? Practice your skills with this simple continuous-line design. Begin stitching at the • and follow the arrows until the design is completed. Remember to watch the line of the design and not the needle. One more time, don't forget to breathe.

Begin here

Quilting Health

In our enthusiasm to finish projects with our machine quilting, we sometimes overlook a few simple things we should do to make it a more enjoyable and healthier process. Consider:

Lighting

The lights on many sewing machines are not adequate for extended periods of machine quilting. You need to see your marks clearly so you can stitch with confidence. Additional lamps positioned to eliminate strong shadows are a big help. Another trick to help avoid eye strain is to lift your head frequently and focus your eyes on another part of the room.

Chair

If your chair is the wrong height and size for you, your back and shoulders will be under strain. Quilters differ in the positions they are comfortable sitting when quilting. If you like to lean into your machine, make sure your chair is high enough, or sit on pillows. A good secretarial chair is nice because it allows you to push away from your machine without having to lift your chair. The best chair height also takes into consideration the distance your eyes need to focus on the area around the needle.

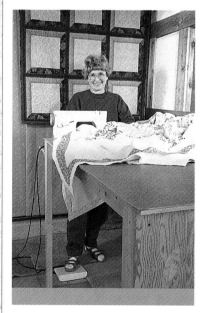

Standing

Standing while you quilt might be an answer for you. I stand while I quilt (especially large quilts) and find it much easier and more relaxing because I have better leverage handling the quilt. Also, it is easier to walk away for a minute or two because you don't have to get up—you are already up. You automatically move around more. Rearranging a quilt also seems to take less effort. My table is at a height comfortable for my arms and my focal length for quilting. It is wide enough to support the quilt and positioned so that the quilt cannot fall away from the table. This table was made for me by my partner/husband Gordon.

Break Time

Just because you are machine quilting does not mean you should finish a queen-size quilt in a day. Even if you are stitching under a horrid deadline (births and weddings are rarely planned with the quilter in mind) be good to yourself and take frequent breaks to relax.

Fantastic Beginning

34" x 34"   **Made by Cheryl Osborn**

Cheryl Osborn chose the Fantasy pattern, shown on page 36 for her first quilt. For the trapunto batt she used Fairfield's Ultra Loft® and for the final batt she used Cotton Classic®, another batt by Fairfield. The quilting was done with cotton thread.

Feathered Friend II

*86" x 86"   **Made by Sue Danielson***

The quilting design duet, Delight and Double Delight, pages 64 and 65, was designed for quilts that need two designs that flow into one another, such as this feathered star. Sue used three layers of Hobb's Heirloom® Cotton with 100% cotton thread for the trapunto batt and also used Heirloom Cotton for the final quilting.

86" x 86"   ***Made by Hari Walner***

Irish Tenors

Hari Walner used the Birdsong design on page 49. The trapunto batt was Fairfield's Ultra Loft and the final batt was Fairfield's Cotton Classic. Although the stippling behind the motifs and into the adjoining pieced blocks added texture to the quilt, the quilting design would have been more effective if the birds had been enlarged or if the stippling had been tighter.

As it is, the legs and beaks are sometimes lost in the stippling. (As long as we keep living, we keep learning.) Pieced by Shirley Wegert.

The Lessons

For the most part, these lessons in machine trapunto, stippling, and texture build on each other. Stipple quilting is the subject of Lesson 1 because the designs in all the other lessons will be enhanced with stipple or background quilting. The basic machine trapunto technique is explained in Lesson 2 because that understanding is needed for the techniques that follow in the other lessons.

All of these lessons call for free-motion quilting skills but, as you will see, the initial step in the basic trapunto technique is a great way to practice free-motion quilting because those stitches are not permanent. Explore these ideas, push them to newer levels. Your quilts are getting to be more fun already.

···Equipment···

To do these six lessons you need the following basic machine quilting equipment and supplies.

- Sewing machine.
- Jeans/denim needles #70 for embroidery thread.
- Machine embroidery needle #75 for use with basting thread, if your thread frays.
- Machine embroidery thread, 50 weight.
- Water-soluble basting thread such as Wash-A-Way™.
- Darning or quilting foot for free-motion quilting.
- Blunt-end scissors. Children's scissors with the rounded points that Fiskars™ makes work great for cutting away trapunto batt.

- Fabric for top and backing.
- Batting: thick polyester batt for most of the trapunto methods, and cotton or cotton-blend batting (strongly recommended) for your final quilting. Cotton and cotton blends are much easier to machine quilt. Keep your life simple.
- A smile on your face and an adventurous spirit. You wouldn't be interested in this book if you weren't already very creative.

Lesson 1
Stipple Quilting

Lesson 2
Machine Trapunto

Lesson 3
Backtracking over Stitches

Lesson 4
Shading with Stitches

Lesson 5
Two-Layer Trapunto

Lesson 6
Shadow Trapunto

Lesson One

Stipple Quilting
and Other Background Effects

Staying in the Background

One of the beautiful aspects of stipple quilting is the way the light travels on top of the little ridges between the lines of stitching. Stippling is a free-motion quilting technique.

If you densely quilt areas next to motifs, those areas will have the effect of being in the background and cause the motifs to appear to come forward. There are several lovely techniques to quilt a background. You can easily figure out a system for doing most of them, but stipple quilting presents other challenges. In our now-developing machine quilting language, stipple quilting has come to be understood as a gracefully meandering and wandering line of stitching used mainly in the background of a design.

Although this lesson will concentrate on how to do your own stipple quilting, the photos below show the appearance and effect of several other background quilting techniques. The practice design for this lesson is Hmmm! Delicious on page 31.

Grid quilting

The straight lines of grid quilting can be an excellent background. Many different styles and sizes of grids can be used. Shown is a simple grid drawn on the diagonal of the design. Use a walking foot and a parallel guide for grid quilting.

Scallop quilting

When stitched closely together, scallops can be effective as a background. This is much easier when done as a free-motion technique. Use coins as templates for drawing the scallops.

Loop and loop quilting

This background is similar to stipple quilting, except that loops are stitched as you wander, and little dots of light on top of the loops mingle with the lines of light on the ridges. This seems to give a playful, or more casual effect. Use free-motion quilting for this technique.

Echo quilting

This type of quilting is just what it says. It echoes the motifs it surrounds. Using a free-motion technique, stitch around the quilting or appliqué motif that you want to enhance, following the shape of the motif. You can keep each succeeding "echo" an equal distance from the previous one, or you can slightly increase the spacing between the echoes.

Background Density

When you decide on which background technique is best for your project, think about appropriate spacing, or density, of the lines of stitches. Small quilted motifs will get lost in a background that is loosely quilted. The denser the quilting, the more the area appears to recede; but very dense quilting over a large area is not only time consuming, it also causes that area to be more rigid than looser stippling. This might be a consideration when quilting areas of a bed quilt that need to drape well at the bed corners.

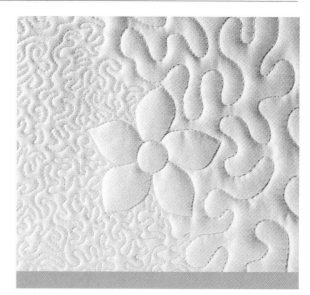

How To Stipple Your Special Quilt

The main idea behind this lesson is to help you develop a method that will allow you to stipple quilt an area of any shape and with whatever density you choose. Stipple quilting is lots of fun, but beware; it is like eating peanuts. Once you start, it is hard to stop.

The great escape. Try not to cross over previous stitches when stipple quilting because that would cut off the line of light that bobs and weaves along the tops of the ridges that form between the curved lines of stitching. To avoid crossing over, we plan "escape routes."

Getting started. Another problem to avoid is the pleats, puckers, and tight ridges that form if we just start at one side of an area and squiggle over to the far side. If you start stitching around the edge of an area and work your way to the center, you will end up with an unwanted balloon bunched up in the center.

Divide and conquer. To eliminate cross-overs and pleats, try this method of subdivide and escape. The area illustrated is an odd shape so you can see how the method can be adapted to any shape or size of area that you want to stipple.

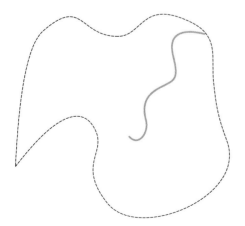

1 Stitch a curvy worm right into the center of the area. Do not stitch all the way to the other side.

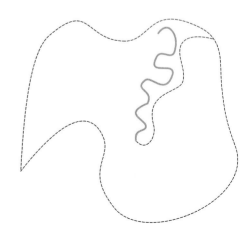

2 Loosely parallel that worm. Now your area is divided into two major sections. Continue stippling the area on the side of the worm. Since you did not stitch all the way to the other side with this first worm, you will have an escape route to the other side.

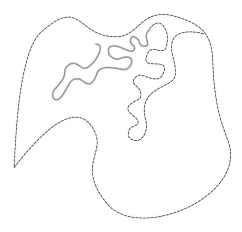

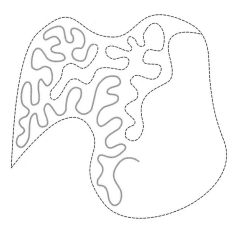

3 Continue to re-subdivide that side of the area into smaller areas with smaller worms. Always leave escape routes by never stitching all the way to the edge of an area. The subdividing will distribute the fabric and the batting, and the escape routes will allow you to keep stitching without having to go over previous lines of stitches.

4 When you have finished stippling the first side of the original worm, use the escape route that you left at the edge of the area to stitch over to the other side. Sometimes you subdivide and escape at the same time with just a single loop.

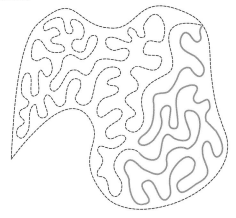

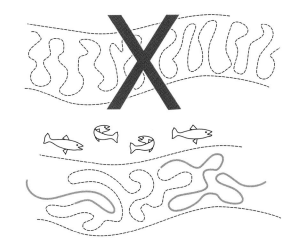

5 Stitch the other major section in the same manner. Plan to finish your stippling so that you can continue on with your quilting, either to stitch another line or to stipple another area.

STIPPLING A LONG, NARROW CHANNEL.
When stippling a long narrow shape, don't just stitch from edge to edge as you travel down the channel. This will push the fabric and batting ahead of your needle, and sooner or later you will have a pleat. Make short subdivisions down the middle and double back, much as a fish swims a river.

Stitch Length

The length of stitches for your stippling will depend on how soft or sharp you like to stitch your curves and arcs. Long stitches will prevent you from being able to turn smaller, graceful curves. Small, uneven stitches might be a distraction. The length of stitch you like for the rest of your quilting will probably be the best for your stippling. Remember, stipple quilting is usually done to give a background effect and as such it should not detract from the main motifs. Very good stippling should be the last element on the quilt to be noticed.

Spacing

There are no rules, and there shouldn't be, about how close or far apart your stippling lines should be from each other. Small scale projects with small motifs and small background areas to quilt call for closer stippling. Miniature quilts certainly call for miniature stippling. It is easy to envision large arcs and shapes stippled on expressive new quilts. If your quilt calls for consistent, even stippling, moderate in density, then that should be your goal. Most important is for you to choose a density that you feel is appropriate for your quilt art, and to do it well. We are not quilt-by-number quilters.

···Helpful Hints···

■ To stipple quilt evenly, stitch at a steady pace. Sometimes, when stippling is going well, the tendency is to try to "get on with it," and we unconsciously begin to move the quilt faster. If you move the quilt faster without speeding up the motor of your machine, you will get larger loops and curves that will be inconsistent with what you have already stitched. Keep a steady pace.

■ To build your confidence and develop your own sense of stipple quilting, use a paper and pencil and "stipple." Practice subdividing and planning escape routes.

■ If you have a particular project in mind, draw the shape and size of the area that you want to stipple on paper and practice with your pencil. This should not necessarily be an exact pattern for you to follow, but it will give you an excellent idea of how to plan that area when you are at your sewing machine.

Hmmm! Delicious

7" Block

If this is your first attempt at stipple quilting, you might want to trace the background of the apple onto a piece of paper and practice with a pencil.

1 Mark all lines of the Hmmm! Delicious pattern on the quilt top. Stitch the apple first. Begin at the • and follow the arrows.

2 Stitch the inside line of the scallops next, beginning at the •.

3 The arrows will show you how to stitch the worm in the same continuous line. When you complete the inside of the scallops, you have the option either to cross over and stitch the outside line of the scallops, or stipple quilt the background of the apple and worm and then cross over and stitch the outside line.

Lesson Two

Machine Trapunto

I Can't Take Another Stitch, I'm Stuffed

For years quilters have taken enormous amounts of time to painstakingly make tiny holes in the backs of their quilts and then stuff selected quilted motifs with additional batting. Then these super quilters carefully sewed these splits closed. That method is the traditional trapunto method, done to add texture and depth, much like bas-relief sculpture. It is a beautiful effect. We love the look. We love the feel. We don't have the time. We sigh.

Now you can achieve a wonderful trapunto look in your quilts, in much less time, without having to make small cuts or holes in the backs of your quilts. And you can use your sewing machine to quilt this technique. This lesson will explain the basic idea of machine trapunto. This lesson will make you sing with ideas.

Materials

■ A thick, heavy polyester batt and your favorite regular batt
(I prefer to use a cotton or cotton-blend batt for my regular batt).

■ Water-soluble basting thread.

■ Blunt-end scissors.

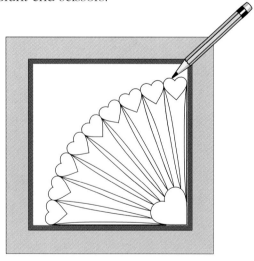

This demonstration uses the Fantasy design (page 36).

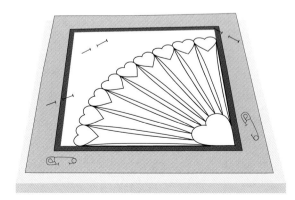

1 Trace all black lines of the Fantasy quilting design onto your quilt top.

2 Pin a very thick batt (a dense polyester batt works well) to the wrong side of your quilt top. You can use straight pins or safety pins. Do not use a quilt backing at this time.

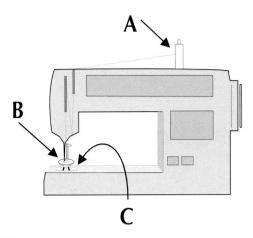
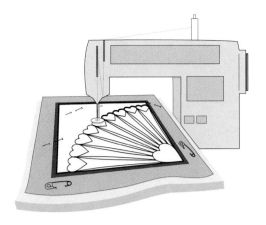

3 (A) Thread your machine with water soluble thread. Use regular light colored thread in the bobbin.

(B) Attach a darning or quilting foot to your machine.

(C) Drop the feed dogs.

4 Using free-motion quilting with the water-soluble thread, stitch on the black line that is adjacent to the red line on the design. Follow the directional diagram A on page 36. Do not stitch any of the other black lines.

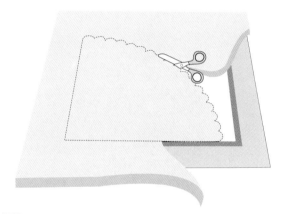
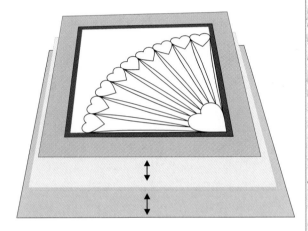

5 Turn the quilt top over. Use your blunt-end scissors and cut away the batt from the areas that you do not want to appear stuffed. Cut as close as you can to the stitched line.

6 After the polyester batt is trimmed away from the background of the fan, you can treat your quilt top as you usually do at this point. Layer it with your regular batting (cotton or cotton-blend batting will work best here) and quilt backing.

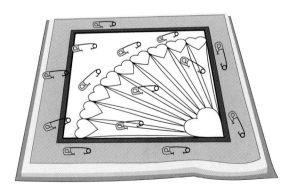
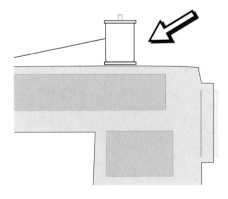

7 Pin baste your quilt top with safety pins. Your fabric may be somewhat puckered in areas. Pin baste very securely, using extra pins right next to and through the patches of thick batt.

8 IMPORTANT STEP! Return your regular thread to your sewing machine. Do not forget this step.

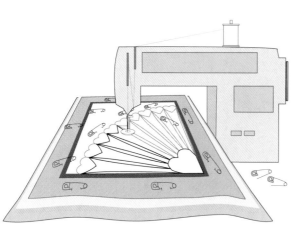

9 Following diagram B on page 36 that accompanies the Fantasy design, stitch all lines of the design with free-motion techniques. Some of your stitching will be on top of the stitches that you made previously with the water-soluble thread. Do not worry if your stitches are not exactly on top of those stitches, because those first stitches will be dissolved.

10 To further enhance the trapunto look, fill the background with a compacting background stitch such as echo quilting or stipple quilting.

11 When you have completed all your quilting and have put the binding on your quilt, immerse your quilt in clear, tepid water. Let it sit for a minute or two and agitate it by hand for five to ten seconds. This will dissolve the water-soluble basting thread. If you have used a water-soluble marker this immersion will also cause the marks to disappear. Dry your quilt flat and shape it if necessary.

That is the basic machine trapunto technique. Now when you are trying to fall asleep but your head keeps designing quilts, you can add another dimension.

···Helpful Hints···

■ Good quality, tightly woven fabrics withstand the stress of the added thick batt better than loosely woven fabrics.

■ Use a cotton or a cotton-blend for your final batt. It clings to fabric, doesn't slip and shift, and is much easier to machine quilt than polyester batts.

■ Take the time to pin baste your final quilt sandwich very securely. This is extremely important when doing this technique.

■ A thick batt can be awkward to handle, so don't pin a large piece to the back of an entire quilt top. Cut and stitch smaller pieces on the back of your quilt where you want the trapunto effect. If you are going to trapunto many elements of a block, cut a piece of thick batt the size of the block. If you stitch and trim the thick batt from each block as you go, you will eliminate bulk and your quilt top will be easier to handle. When doing a larger quilt, trim away excess batt frequently to make the quilt top easier to handle.

■ Although it is tempting to baste the thick batt onto single patches before piecing, try to avoid this. Smaller patches with raw edges are more likely to pucker because of the tension caused when the thick batt is stitched onto the back. This possible puckering can affect the way those patches fit to other patches. Instead, sew at least some of the surrounding patches to the patch that will be trapuntoed. It is usually easier to put the whole top together and then baste the pieces of thick batt to areas you want trapuntoed.

■ When Linda Graham does this technique, she likes to stitch all the quilting lines of the trapuntoed areas with the water-soluble thread. She says it is easier to do her final quilting because the lines in the thick batt are already compressed. Experiment and see what works best for you.

NOTE: From this point on, the quilting patterns in this book have red lines adjacent to some of the black lines. These lines indicate where your line of stitching will be when you stitch the thick trapunto batt with water-soluble thread.

Fantasy
6¹/₂" Block

1 Mark all lines of the Fantasy pattern on the quilt top.

2 With the thick batt behind the fan, stitch with water-soluble basting thread on the black line next to the red line on the pattern (A). Cut batt away from background of fan.

3 Make your quilt sandwich.

4 Change to regular thread. Begin stitching the design at the • and follow the arrows to quilt the fan (B). When you finish stitching the fan, follow the arrow into the background and stipple.

Stipple quilting is an excellent way to accent the fan, but this design is also nice with echo quilting. (See *Fantastic Beginning* on page 23.)

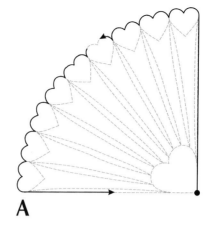

A

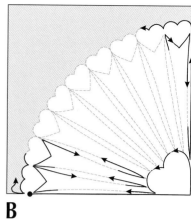

B

Lesson Three

Backtracking Over Stitches

A Short Lesson in Covering Your Tracks

■ **After you become comfortable with backtracking over your stitches, always look for designs that have a well-planned stitching sequence.**

■ **If your eyes become tired, refocus them at something across the room: a favorite object or a painting. The refocusing is good exercise for your eyes, and seeing a pretty object will help you relax.**

For machine quilting, patterns designed with one continous line are the easiest to stitch; but as you progress with your skills, you may want to try designs requiring that you occasionally stitch back over previous stitches for short lines. When you realize that you can do this backtracking you will have the confidence to try many designs that you otherwise might not have considered. One small step in quilting, one giant step for the quilter.

Materials

- Machine quilting thread
- Cotton or cotton-blend batting*

This lesson is about learning to backtrack over previous stitches, but the design is very suitable for the trapunto technique. If you would like to trapunto this design, you will need the supplies listed for Lesson 2.

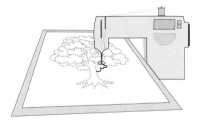

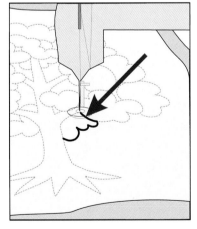

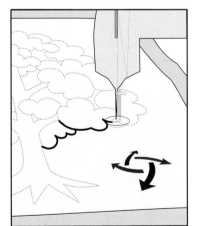

The design for this lesson, Cottonwood, is excellent to practice backtracking. It is beautifully accented with background quilting.

The only thing you need to keep in mind when stitching back over previously made stitches is to remember to look at the stitches you are about to stitch over, not at the needle. The needle is not moving, but the quilt is. Look three or four stitches down the road. With a little practice, this skill will be yours.

Cottonwood
10¹/₂" Block

1 Mark all lines of the Cottonwood pattern on the quilt top.

2 Make your quilt sandwich.

3 There are eight lines to this design. Stitch the numbered lines in sequence, beginning at the circled number and ending at the ■ .

Don't be shy. Although this design requires backtracking over previous stitches, you can do it with a little practice. Just remember to always *look at the stitches in front of the needle, not at the needle.*

Lines 4-8

○ Begin
■ Finish

Double lines indicate where you will stitch directly on top of previous stitiches.

Lines 1-3

Lesson Four

Shading with Stitches

The Quilting Lady of Shady Lane

You can use quilting stitches much the way an artist uses pen and ink to give objects additional depth. All you need is a plan and a suitable motif. Not all designs are candidates for this technique, but often there are parts of designs that you can shade.

The trick is to look at the object you are considering shading and then think about where the light would ***not*** be falling directly. These are the areas that you might be able to shade with stitches. The center of a flower is a good example. It is shielded from the light by the outer petals. Dense stitching in the area of the petals near the center of the flower will give shape to the petal. The shaded area will appear to recede.

The following drawings show areas within designs that have been shaded with stitches. Free-motion techniques are used in shading.

Materials

- Machine quilting thread

- Cotton or cotton-blend batting*

Baby Rose (page 42) is a good design to practice this lesson. Stitching sequences are shown in the directional diagrams accompanying the design.

Since the lines of stitching that you use to shade are very much like lines used in pen and ink drawings, these lines of stitching will be called shading stitches. With this shading technique you will often backtrack over three or four previous stitches.

*This design can also be used with the trapunto technique. If you choose to do trapunto you will need the supplies listed in Lesson 2.

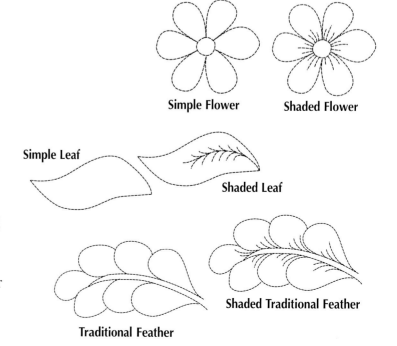

Simple Flower　　　**Shaded Flower**

Simple Leaf

Shaded Leaf

Traditional Feather

Shaded Traditional Feather

To shade a motif with your quilting, just take a few stitches in the area to be shaded, backtrack over those stitches, stitch to the next shade line, and repeat the process, over and over again, until that area recedes the way you want it to. The following will demonstrate shading the area outlined in the drawing shown at right.

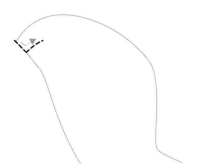

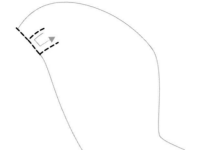

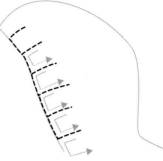

1 Stitch on the design line of the area to be shaded until you want to add shading. Take a few shading stitches into that area.

2 Backtrack over those few shading stitches back to the line of the design. Take a few more stitches on the design line and then make another shading line.

3 Backtrack over this line. Continue stitching one shading line after another until the area is shaded to your taste and it looks good to you.

The shading is done at the same time that the overall design is being stitched, and is part of the final quilting.

You do not need to mark the lines of shading on your quilt top. Your shading lines will never be the same, even on the same motif. Some will be a stitch or two longer, some at slightly different angles. Don't make yourself crazy. It will be enough just to plan ahead where you would like to put some of these lines.

···Helpful Hints···

■ Do not shade an area adjacent to where you will be doing any background quilting. The shading will blend into the background. This blending of background and object may be desirable in some instances, but it will detract from the object you are shading. Also, don't shade an area next to another shaded area. You will lose the definition in both areas.

■ Do not make the lines of shading very long. A few stitches go a long way in adding depth.

■ When doing this technique with the trapunto technique, you will stitch your thick trapunto batt first. Shading is a nice complement to trapunto.

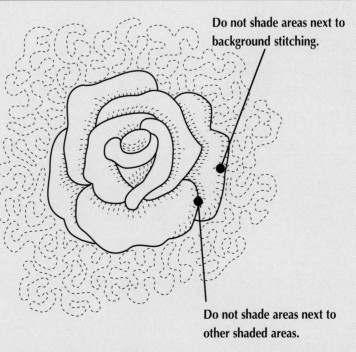

Do not shade areas next to background stitching.

Do not shade areas next to other shaded areas.

Baby Rose
5" Block

Baby Rose is an excellent design to practice the shading technique. The lines of shading that are shown are only suggestions as to where or how many shading lines you might stitch.

1 Mark all the lines of the Baby Rose pattern on the quilt top.

2 Make your quilt sandwich.

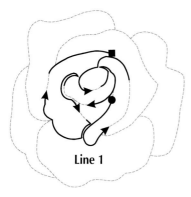

Line 1

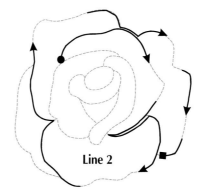

Line 2

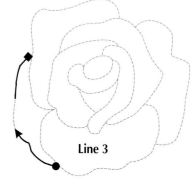

Line 3

3 Begin stitching each line of Baby Rose at the •. Each line will end at the ■. There are some lines where you will be stitching back over previous lines of stitching.

If you want to use the shading technique, make the stitches as you stitch the line they are attached to, as shown in Lesson 4.

If you want to trapunto Baby Rose, baste the thick batt with water-soluble thread on the black line that is adjacent to the red line.

Lesson Five

Two-Layer Trapunto

Watch Out, Rodin!

If you want even more of a sculpted, stuffed effect than you get with the techniques in Lesson 2, you can add a second layer of batting to selected areas. This second layer can add an extra snap to your quilt. It can also look like a bas-relief sculpture.

The principle of this lesson is much the same as in Lesson Two. The basic idea is just carried one step further.

Materials

- Thick polyester batt and cotton or cotton-blend batt

- Water-soluble basting thread

- Blunt-end scissors

Practice this lesson using the Fruitful Basket (page 46). The photographs will demonstrate how to add even more dimension to some of the grapes, one cherry, and the apple in front of the basket. This is how the technique is done.

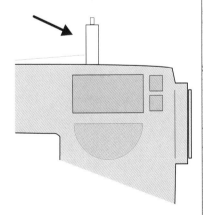

1 Mark all the black lines of the Fruitful Basket on your quilt top. Pin pieces of thick batting to the back of the quilt top behind the areas outlined in green on the pattern.

The back of your quilt top might look something like this.

2 Use water-soluble basting thread as the top thread of your machine and regular light-colored thread in the bobbin. Drop or cover your feed dogs and attach a darning or quilting foot to your machine.

3 Free-motion stitch on the black line that is adjacent to the green line.

4 Turn the quilt top over and, with blunt-end scissors, cut away the excess batt that is outside the stitched lines. At this point you will have three patches of thick batt sewn and trimmed.

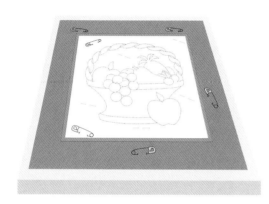

5 Pin another piece of thick batt to the back of the quilt top. This piece of batt should cover the entire basket and front apple.

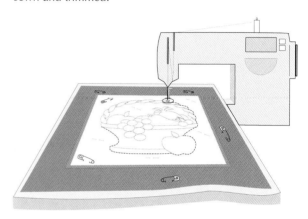

6 Continue to use the water-soluble basting thread in the needle. This time free-motion stitch on the black lines that are adjacent to the red lines.

7 Again, turn your quilt top over and trim away the excess batt. Now you have a larger piece of thick batt stitched to the back of your design. At this point there are two layers of batt behind some of the grapes, one cherry, and the apple in front of the basket.

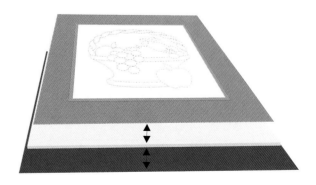

8 Now you can treat your quilt top as you would a regular quilt top. Layer it with your favorite cotton batting and quilt backing. Safety-pin baste the quilt sandwich very securely. Use extra pins around the areas that have the thick batt in back of them. These areas often pucker a little.

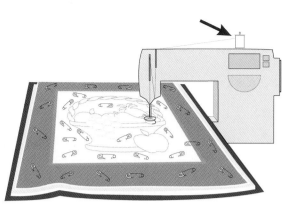

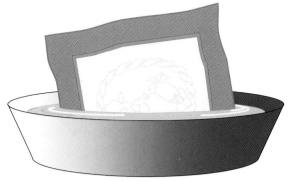

9 **With your regular machine quilting thread back in the machine,** free-motion quilt all of the black lines in the design. Background quilting makes the design stand out even more.

10 When your quilt is completely quilted and bound, immerse it in clear water to remove the basting thread and markings.

TIPS

■ **The thicker the batt you use, the more distortion and puckering you can expect in your fabric.**

■ **Stitch slowly when using the water-soluble thread. This thread is not made for strength and stitching through the thick polyester batt(s) can cause fraying. If your thread frays excessively, try using a machine embroidery needle.**

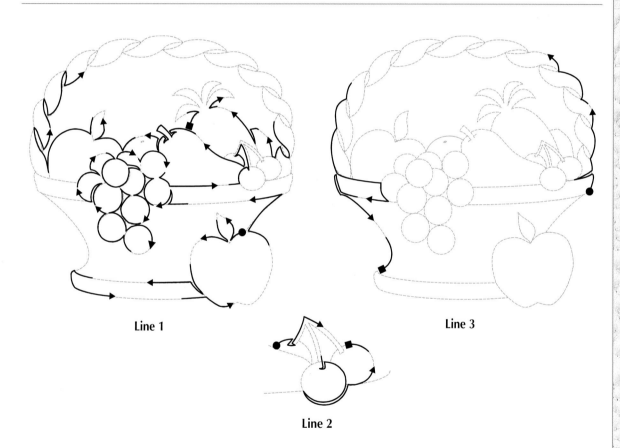

Line 1

Line 2

Line 3

Begin stitching each line at the •. Each line of stitching will end at the ■. There will be times when you will be stitching back over previous lines of stitching.

Stitching Directions for Fruitful Basket Design, page 46.

Fruitful Basket
7 1/2" Block

If you are doing two-layer trapunto, first baste thick batting using the green line as a stitching guide. Follow the step-by-step directions in Lesson 5.

If you want to trapunto this design in one layer, stitch the thick batt onto the back of the block with water-soluble thread on the black line adjacent to the red line and trim the batt outside that line.

Lesson Six

Shadow Trapunto

The Shadow Shows...

This lesson combines two quilting worlds: trapunto and shadow appliqué. By using both these techniques we add the depth of trapunto to the subtleties of shadow work. It is a lovely marriage.

Prepare your sewing machine for free-motion quilting. The practice design for this lesson, Birdsong, is on page 49.

Materials

- A good quality, tightly woven, sheer, light-weight, solid-colored fabric. Good choices are lawn cottons and high quality batistes. The fabric must be strong, but sheer enough to see a darker fabric through it.

- Dark colored fabric to cover the back of the block.

- Quilt backing.

- Water-soluble basting thread, regular machine quilting thread.

- Cotton or cotton-blend batting. A cotton or cotton blend batt is recommended even for the trapunto part of this technique because of its opacity.

- Blunt-end scissors.

1 Mark all the lines of the design on the sheer, solid fabric. Pin a white, opaque cotton or cotton-blend batting to the back of the quilt top.

2 Using water-soluble basting thread, free-motion stitch on the black lines of the design that are adjacent to the red lines. Follow Diagram A that accompanies the Birdsong design (Page 49).

■ **Cotton and cotton-blend batts are more opaque than polyester batts and work best for the trapunto part of this technique. Exception: The cotton batts with the seeds do not work well because the seeds will show through the sheer fabric.**

■ **Experiment with using a slightly darker thread when doing this technique, especially if you decide to do any background quilting. A thread lighter than the grayish tone of the background would detract from the illusion of depth.**

Back of Quilt

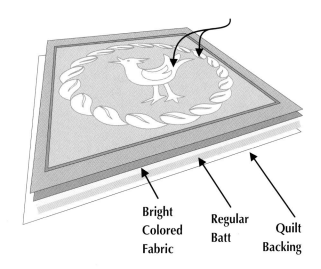

Bright Colored Fabric   Regular Batt   Quilt Backing

3 Turn your quilt top over. With blunt-end scissors, trim the batt away from areas you want shadowed (darkened). Trim closely, because with the sheer fabric on top, any white batt you leave behind will show through. In this design leave the cotton batt behind the bird and the leaf wreath.

4 When the entire quilt top has been trapunto basted and trimmed, layer the quilt top with a piece of bright or dark-colored fabric, regular batt, and backing. Be sure that the bright piece of fabric covers all the area of the back that you want shadowed, and that it is face up between the quilt top and the regular batt. Check for stray thread that may be on top of the dark fabric and visible through the sheer fabric.

Cut the bright fabric away from the back of the quilt top in all areas other than those made of sheer fabric. This excess fabric is unnecessary and will only add bulk. Baste entire quilt top securely with safety pins.

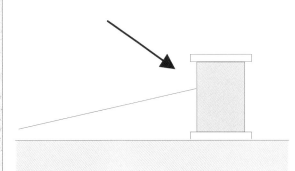

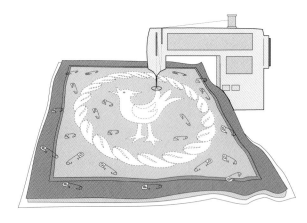

5 Return regular machine quilting thread to the needle of the machine.

6 Free-motion quilt all the lines of the design. This time follow the stitching directions shown in Diagram B.

At this point the design is well defined, but it is enhanced even more with background quilting.

When all quilting is complete and you have attached your binding, immerse your quilt in clear, tepid water to dissolve water-soluble basting thread.

Birdsong

7¹/₂" Circle
4¹/₂" wide Bird

A

When you baste the first cotton batt to the back of your quilt top with water-soluble basting thread, follow Diagram A.

B

Diagram B is for the final quilting. You may begin anywhere on the bird and stitch in one continuous line. When you stitch the ring of leaves, stitch the inner line first starting at the •, including the veins of the leaves. Then cross over and stitch the outer line ending at the ■. Stitching the inner line first will help avoid puckering.

*41" x 54"   **Made by Lynette Fulton***

Judy's Star

Starry-Eyed, page 66, is the quilting pattern Lynette chose for her quilt. The piecing design is from Trudie Hughes' book *Template-Free Quiltmaking*.

The batt she used for the trapunto is Hi-Loft® polyester by Fairfield Processing and the final batt is Cotton Classic, also by Fairfield. Cotton thread was used for quilting.

Traditional Chintz Quilt Without the Traditional Work

Judy machine appliquéd the birds and flowers and used the Quiet Tree pattern on page 70 for the trapunto and quilting design. The pattern was modified for the border. She used Fairfield's polyester Hi-Loft for the trapunto batt and Hobbs Heirloom Cotton for the final batt. The quilting was done with cotton thread.

63" x 63"   ***Made by Judy Morin***

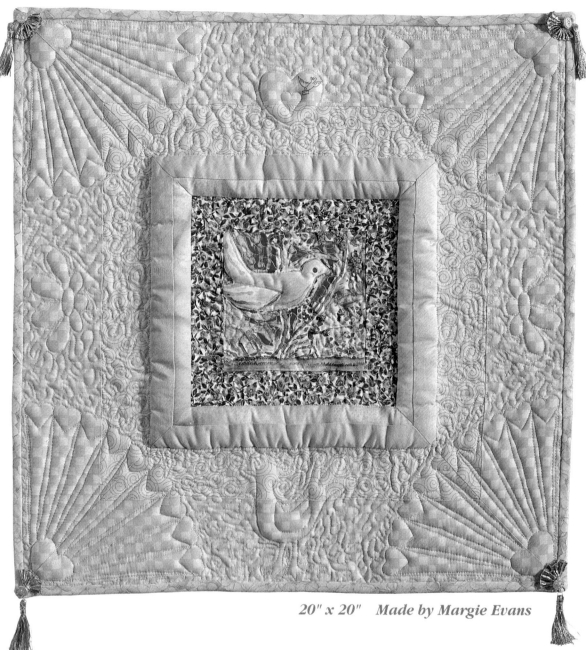

20" x 20"   Made by Margie Evans

Mama's Songbird

Margie used parts of several quilting designs for this little wall cutey: Birdsong, page 49; Fantasy, page 36; Quiet Tree, page 70. Margie used two layers of Fatt Batt® by Mountain Mist for the trapunto batt and Warm and Natural™ 100% cotton for the final batt. Rayon thread was used in the quilting. The center panel was hand painted by Linda Felix Ybarra.

Time to Quilt?

Time does not hide from us, it is always here. When we can't "find" time to quilt it is because we give other activities higher priorities. And these are often activities like earning a living, tending to family, helping a neighbor, fixing the car, eating and sleeping. It is not easy to decide what gets to the head of the line. How can we use time to enjoy our quilting?

In the early sixties I read a book, *The Creative Woman,* by Dorothy Goldberg. This woman was a prolific artist/painter living in the Washington, D.C., area.

She raised three daughters, and her husband Arthur was deeply involved in politics on a national level. With the demands of raising her children and being a political partner, she still continued to create wonderful paintings and exhibit frequently.

When asked how she managed, she explained that she always thought of her art as a child, and each child needs time and love. Children need to be fed and hugged. They sometimes need to be taken to a doctor, or to dance lessons, or to softball practice. When her first daughter arrived, she considered that she then had two children, and she always knew she would have time for each child as it came along.

Although I long ago lost the book, I have often thought of her lovely philosophy. Many, many times my "art child" needs nurturing, and the time is there.

Spring Quintet
7¹/₂" or 15" Blocks

Techniques to consider for this design:

■ **Lesson 1**
Stipple Quilting
■ **Lesson 2**
Machine Trapunto
■ **Lesson 6**
Shadow Trapunto

Spring Quintet mixes a little of the perkiness of Spring and the elegance of a drawing room. Cheryl Phillips's shadow quilt on page 87 is stitched using this quilting design.

This design can be used on point, or you can put four designs together, each turned 90°, for a 15" design. The diagram on the facing page shows what the 15" design looks like.

A

1 If you are using the trapunto technique (Lesson 2), follow Diagram A, beginning and ending at the • when basting the thick batt with water-soluble thread. Note that you do not stitch the inside of the heart, the centers of the side motifs, the base of the flowers, or the inner flower lines with the water-soluble thread.

2 Diagram B shows to cut the thick batt away from the areas shown in gray.

C

First stitch line 1, then line 2.

3 Follow Diagram C to do your final quilting. This time you will stitch all the detail lines.

Four Spring Quintets, each turned 90°, look like this.

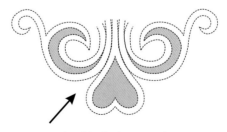

Another option for this design is to also cut away the first batt from the center of the heart and the centers of the two side motifs. Stipple-quilt inside these areas when you stipple the rest of the background. If you prefer that option, when you do your initial stitching with water-soluble thread you must stitch the inner line of the heart and the inner lines of the side motifs.

Swanee
20" Circular Block

Swanee is a large mandala-type design.
Follow the diagrams to make the complete pattern.
Quilts using this design are on pages 81 & 90.

Techniques to consider for this design:

■ **Lesson 1**
Stipple Quilting
■ **Lesson 2**
Machine Trapunto
■ **Lesson 6**
Shadow Trapunto

1 Fold a 22" square of paper in half.

2 Fold in half again.

3 Fold in half diagonally, into eighths.

4 Open and trace Swanee design in each eighth.

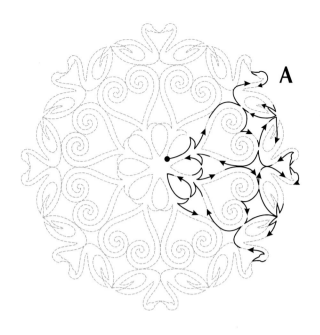

A

If you are using the trapunto technique (Lesson 2), follow Diagram A, beginning and ending at the • when basting the thick batt with the water-soluble basting thread.

B

Diagram B shows to cut the thick batt away from the gray areas. The gray areas in Diagram B can be background quilted.

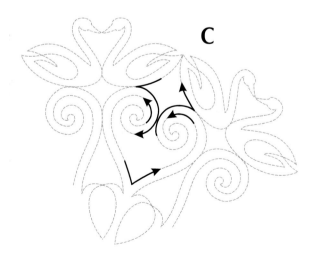

C

Diagram C shows how to stitch the swirls in the centers of the hearts when you do your final quilting.

Options

When using Swanee with the Shadow Trapunto technique (Lesson 6) you might want to baste the lines on the inside of the hearts (diagram C) and cut the batt away from the inside of the hearts when cutting away the thick trapunto batt. This will give you more of the design detail in the shadow effect.

Folk Dance
14" Block, 2½" Border

Folk Dance is a lively pattern that is a good fill for large blocks. It can also be used for a lovely wallhanging. The matching border is on the facing page.

A wall quilt made by Jo Thogode using this pattern is on page 79.

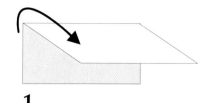

1

2

3

1 Fold a 16" square of paper in half.

2 Fold in half again.

3 Open and trace Folk Dance pattern in each quarter.

Do not stitch these inner lines of leaves when basting the thick trapunto batting. Stitch these lines only when you do your final quilting.

A

B

If you are using the trapunto technique (Lesson 2) for the block and border, follow Diagram A, beginning and ending at the • when basting the thick batt with the water-soluble basting thread and doing the final quilting. The slight exception to this is when you baste the trapunto batt onto the back of the block; note the side diagram that shows that you do not need to stitch the inner line of one type of leaf at this time.

The B diagrams show to cut the thick batt away from the areas shown in gray.

Begin stitching at the •. Stitch the inner line of the border until you stitch back to where you started. Cross over the • and stitch the outer line.

Inner Line

A

B

Techniques to consider for this design:

- **Lesson 1** *Stipple Quilting*
- **Lesson 2** *Machine Trapunto*
- **Lesson 4** *Shading with Stitches*
- **Lesson 6** *Shadow Trapunto*

Iridescent Iris
10" Block

Iridescent Iris would look lovely on a two-block quilt where one of the alternating blocks is a solid color and you need a design that will fill the space.

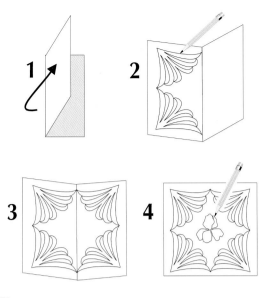

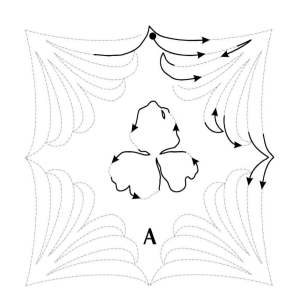

1 Fold a 12" piece of paper in half.

2 Open and trace Iridescent Iris leaf pattern on each half and the Iridescent Iris flower pattern in the center.

3 For the trapunto technique (Lesson 2), follow Diagram A beginning and ending at the • when basting the thick batt with the water-soluble basting thread.

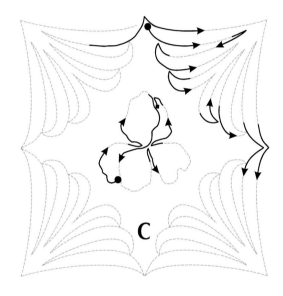

4 Diagram B shows to cut the thick batt away from the areas shown in gray.

5 Follow Diagram C to do the final quilting.

Need a matching border? The leaves surrounding the iris make a lovely border when positioned as shown. You can add the iris, but the leaves alone make a beautiful scalloped border effect.

Over the Rainbow
11" x 5"

Over the
Rainbow

Techniques to consider for this design:

■ **Lesson 1**
Stipple Quilting
■ **Lesson 2**
Machine Trapunto
■ **Lesson 6**
Shadow Trapunto

Embroider, by machine or hand, the interior of the fins, gills, and eye before basting the thick batt with water-soluble thread. If you don't trapunto this fish, embroider it before your make your quilt sandwich.

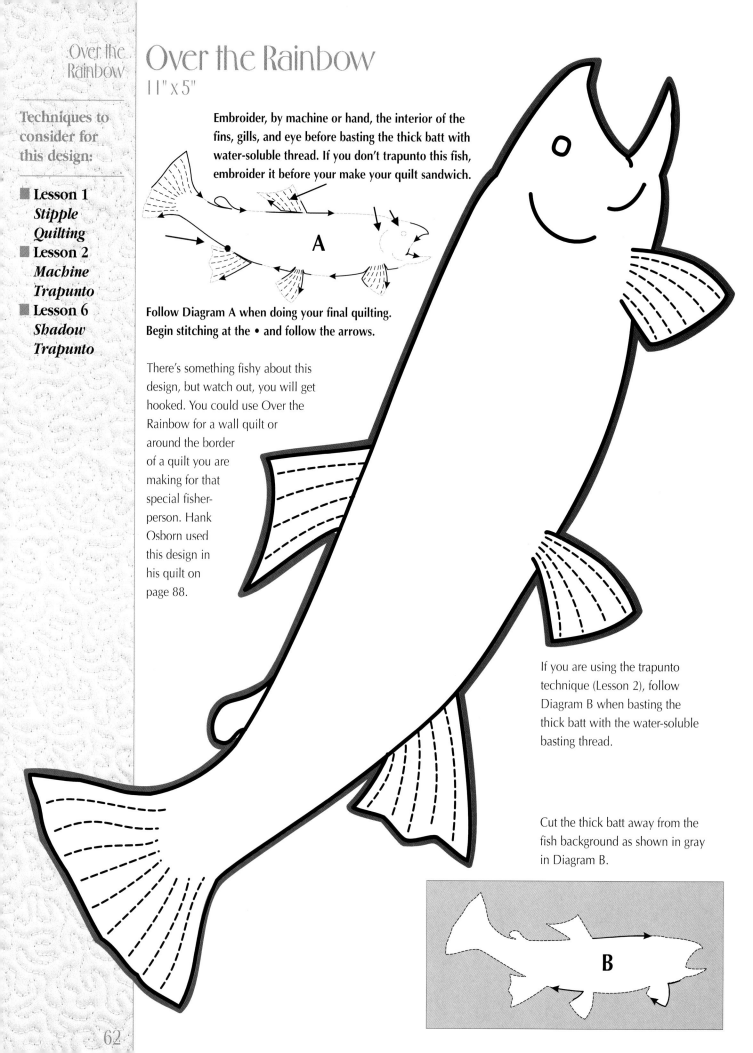

A

Follow Diagram A when doing your final quilting. Begin stitching at the • and follow the arrows.

There's something fishy about this design, but watch out, you will get hooked. You could use Over the Rainbow for a wall quilt or around the border of a quilt you are making for that special fisher-person. Hank Osborn used this design in his quilt on page 88.

If you are using the trapunto technique (Lesson 2), follow Diagram B when basting the thick batt with the water-soluble basting thread.

Cut the thick batt away from the fish background as shown in gray in Diagram B.

B

Simple Manners
11" Block

This design looks fantastic when machine trapuntoed. See Lynette Fulton's experimental/teaching quilt on page 85.

A

If you are using the trapunto technique (Lesson 2), follow Diagram A, beginning and ending at the • when basting the thick batt with the water-soluble basting thread.

If you plan to stipple quilt around this design, stipple these areas as soon as you have enclosed them with your final quilting stitches (Diagram C). Your needle is already there, and you won't have to go back later and fill in those areas.

B

Diagram B shows to cut the thick batt away from the areas shown in gray.

Techniques to consider for this design:

■ **Lesson 1**
Stipple Quilting
■ **Lesson 2**
Machine Trapunto
■ **Lesson 6**
Shadow Trapunto

C

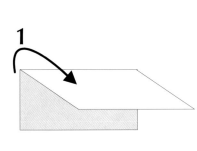

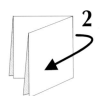

1 Fold a 12" square of paper in half.

2 Fold in half again.

3 Open and trace the Simple Manners pattern on each quarter.

Delight
7" Block

A

B

Double Delight

6" x 7" Block

A

B

For your final quilting, follow the B diagrams, beginning and ending each line of stitching at the • . Stitch inner lines first to avoid puckering. Parts of these designs are similar to traditional feather designs, so there are lines that you will have to stitch back over.

If you are using the trapunto technique (Lesson 2), follow the A diagrams, beginning and ending at the •s when basting the thick batt with the water-soluble basting thread.

Diagram A shows to cut the thick batt away from the areas shown in gray.

If you want to add the shading lines (the dashed lines in gray), stitch them the first time you stitch that line. (See Lesson 4, Shading with Stitches.)

Delight and Double Delight are companion designs. Both shapes fit very well together in quilt patterns such as Feathered Star, where it is nice to have designs that flow into one another. Delight is an excellent fill for a Double Wedding Ring center patch. Sue Danielson's breathtaking quilt on page 24 uses both of these designs.

Techniques to consider for this design:

- ■ **Lesson 1** *Stipple Quilting*
- ■ **Lesson 2** *Machine Trapunto*
- ■ **Lesson 3** *Backtracking over Stitches*
- ■ **Lesson 4** *Shading with Stitches*
- ■ **Lesson 6** *Shadow Trapunto*

Starry-Eyed
7¹/₂" Block, 3" Border

The hearts in this block form a center star, and the matching border gives a heart and scallop effect. See Maureen Newman's quilt on page 82 and Lynette Fulton's quilt on page 85.

Eyed

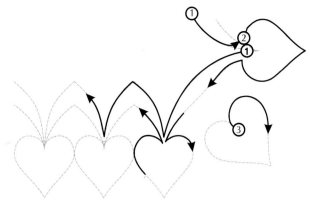

A

If you are using the trapunto technique (Lesson 2), follow the A diagrams beginning and ending at the •s when basting the thick batt with the water-soluble basting thread.

Follow the A diagrams for final quilting. Line 1 is the inner line of the border, and if you stitch that first, you may avoid some puckering. When Line 1 is complete, cross over and stitch Line 2.

Stitch the corner hearts (Line 3) last. If you intend to do any background quilting, the gray areas also suggest where you might want to fill with stippling, echo, or loop and loop.

The B diagrams show to cut the thick batt from areas shown in gray.

B

Susan B. Anthony
7" Block

Susan B. Anthony is similar to Baby Rose (Lesson 4), but it is larger and has an outside row of petals. The two designs are very compatible.

I think we owe Susan B. Anthony and the other wonderful women of the women's suffrage movement a very large rose, and more.

Pacific Rose, Linda Graham's quilt on page 83, uses this design.

1 If you are using the two-layer trapunto technique (Lesson 5), follow Diagram A, basting the thick batt with water-soluble basting thread on the black lines adjacent to green lines.

2 Diagram AA shows to cut the thick batt from areas shown in gray.

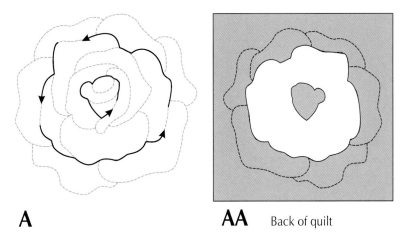

A

AA Back of quilt

3 Pin another piece of thick batt to the back of the rose. Follow Diagram B, basting the thick batt with water-soluble thread on the black line adjacent to the red line.

4 Again, cut the excess batt away from the areas shown in gray on Diagram BB.

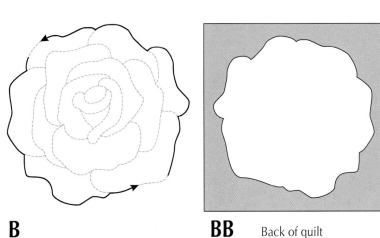

B

BB Back of quilt

5 Follow Diagrams 1, 2, and 3 to do your final quilting. The final quilting is done with only three lines. Begin stitching each line at the • and follow the arrows, ending at the ■. Notice that there are lines where you will backtrack over previous stitches.

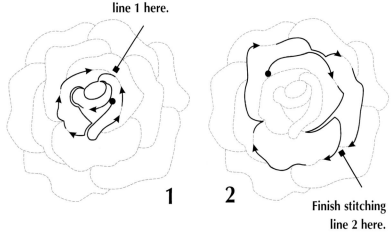

Finish stitching line 1 here.

Finish stitching line 2 here.

1

2

Options

■ If you want to do some shading stitches (Lesson 4), the dashed lines on the pattern indicate areas where you might stitch them.

■ If you only want one layer of trapunto, begin with Step 2. If you don't want to trapunto, begin with Step 3. If you don't want to quilt, write a book.

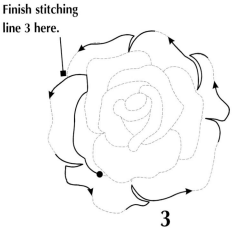

Finish stitching line 3 here.

3

Quiet Tree
7½" and 15" Blocks

Techniques to consider for this design:

- ■ **Lesson 1**
  Stipple Quilting
- ■ **Lesson 2**
  Machine Trapunto
- ■ **Lesson 6**
  Shadow Trapunto

The Quiet Tree design can be used in a block turned on point. By using four Quiet Tree designs, each turned 90°, you can create a 15" design. The 15" design looks very different depending on whether you place the flowers in the center or in the corners.

The variations are illustrated. Ramona Hilton's quilt on page 80, Judy Morin's quilt on page 51, and Danita Rafalovich's quilt on page 84 all use this design.

70

15" Configuration for Quiet Tree

1 Fold a 16" square of paper in half.

2 Fold in half again.

3 Open and trace the Quiet Tree pattern in each section. See illustrations below for two different design options.

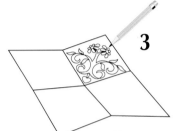

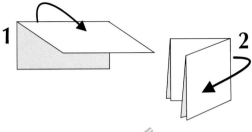

A

If you are using the trapunto technique (Lesson 2), follow the A diagram beginning and ending at the ● when basting the thick batt with the water-soluble basting thread.

Flowers in the center

B

Diagram B shows to cut the thick batt away from the areas shown in gray.

Flowers in the corners

C

Follow Diagram C when you are doing your final quilting beginning and ending at the ●.

Autumn's Treasure
11" Block

For a simple, yet elegant design that fills a block well, this pattern is a treasure. One-quarter of the design is given so it is easy to enlarge or reduce on a photocopy machine to fit your needs.

Margie Evan's quilt on Page 89 uses this design.

A

B

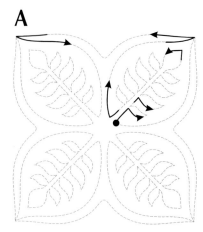

You can use diagram A for stitching with the water soluble basting thread (for machine trapunto) and for your final quilting. Begin and finish stitching at the • .

Diagram B shows where to cut away the thick batt from the area shown in gray for the machine trapunto technique.

1 Fold a 16 " square of paper in half.

2 Fold in half again.

3 Open and trace the pattern given in each quarter.

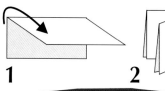
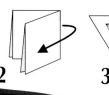

1   **2**   **3**

April's Promise

15½" X 18" Directional diagrams for patterns on page 74-77

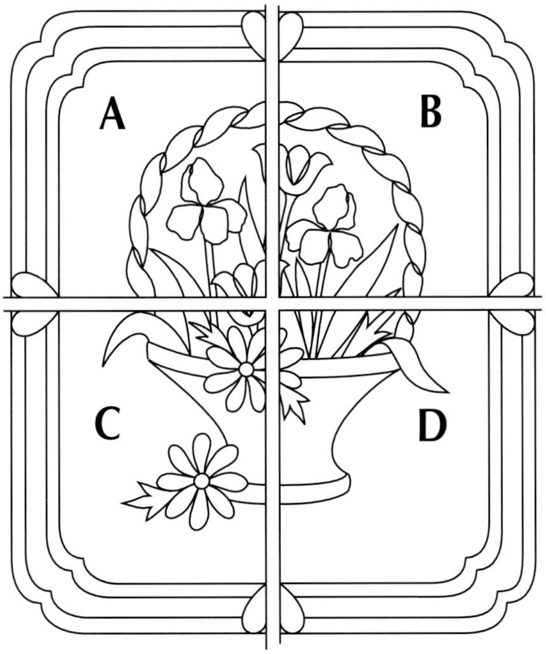

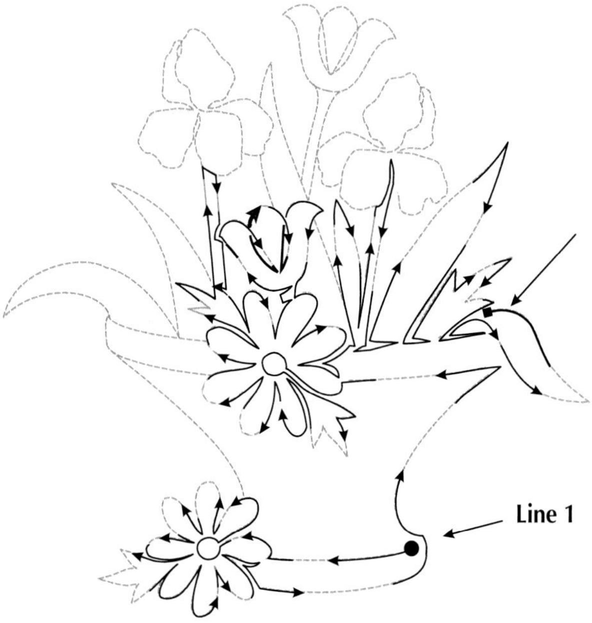

Fold a 17" X 21" piece of paper in half lengthwise and cross wise. Trace each section of April's Promise as shown.

1 Begin stitching at the •. Finish stitching line 1 at the ■. You will need to backtrack over some of your previous stitches.

2 Begin stitching at the • and finish at the ■ for line 2. You will need to backtrack over some of your previous stitches.

3 Lines 3 and 4 are the irises. Begin at the • and finish at the ■.

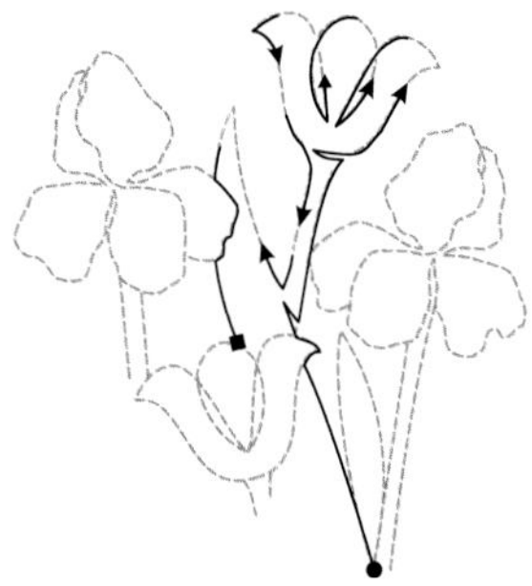

Line 2

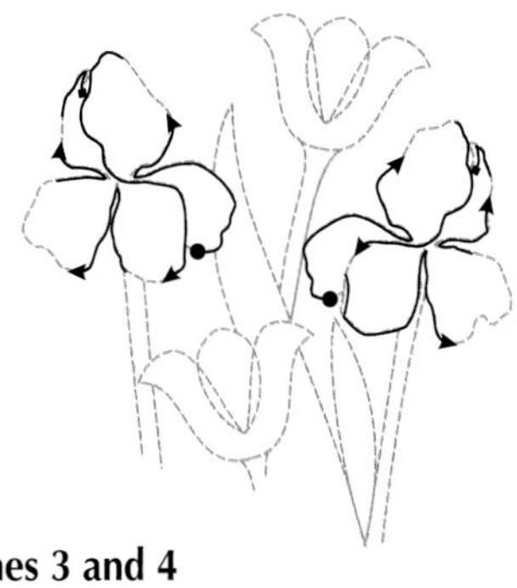

Lines 3 and 4

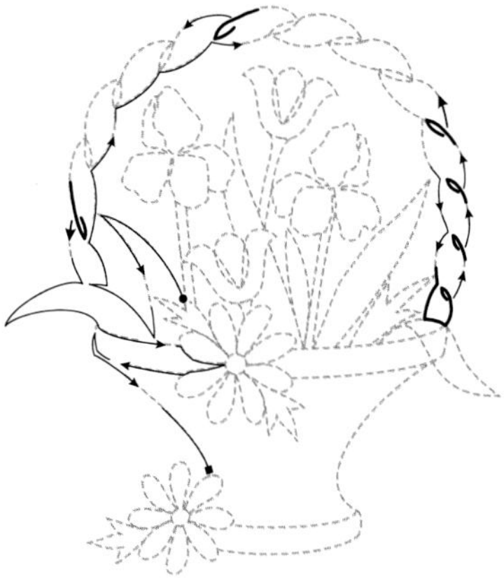

Line 5

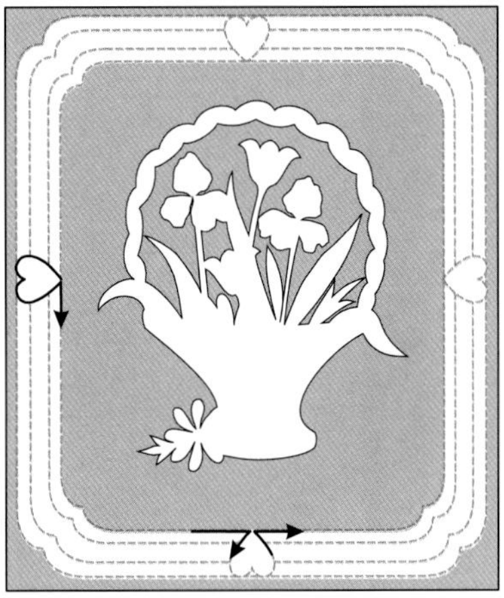

Line 6

4 Begin stitching line 5 at the • and finish at the ■.

5 Stitch Line 6, the inner-most line of the border first, including the hearts. Then stitch the line segments of the next two lines. Finally, stitch the outer line to complete the border.

6 To trapunto: Baste, with water-soluble basting thread, on the red lines of the pattern. (See Lesson 2.) The gray areas show where to cut the batt away. You can stipple quilt the areas shown in gray to accent the design. (See Lesson 1.)

A

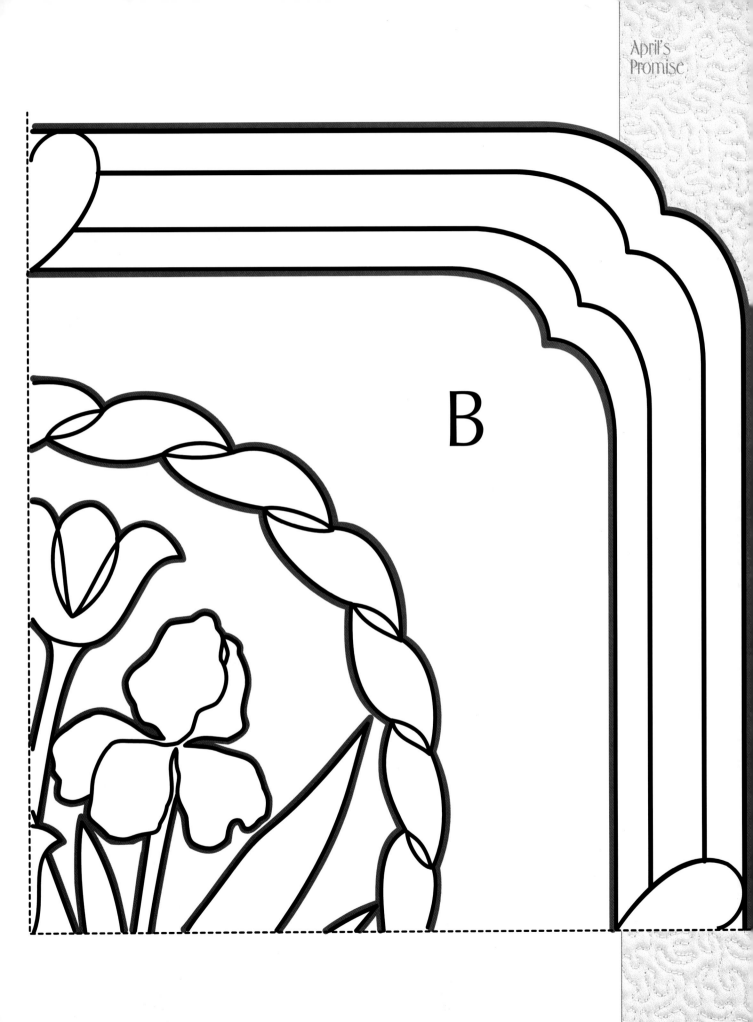

B

C

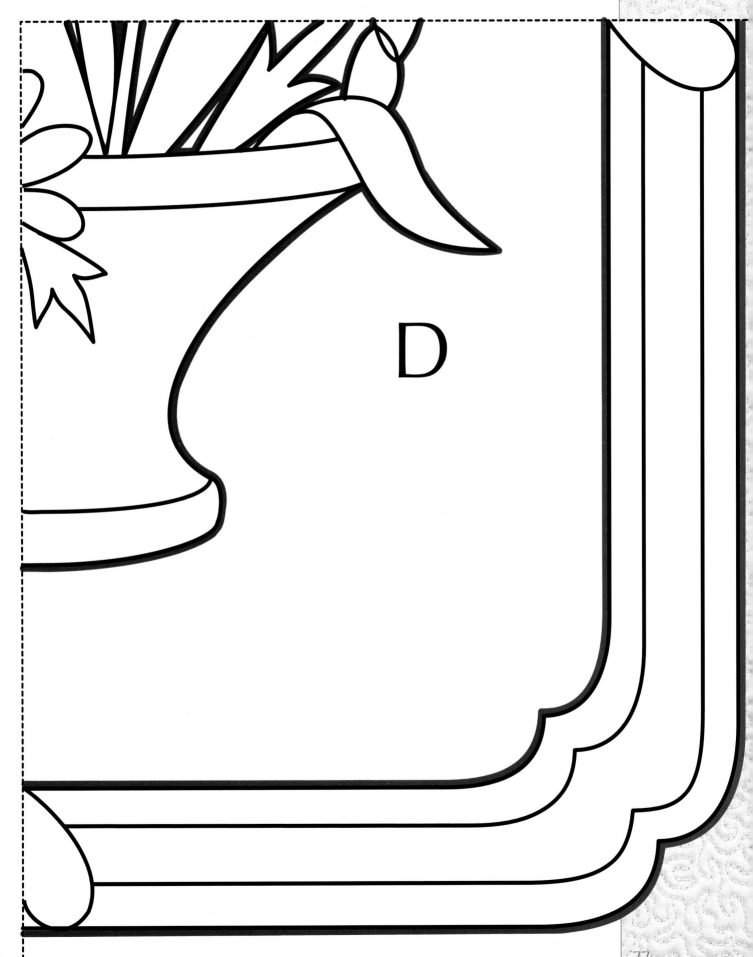

D

April's Promise

19" x 21"   Made by Hari Walner

Design given on pages 74-77
The trapunto batt is a 10 oz. Air-Lite
Synthetic batt and the regular quilting
batt is Cotton Choice by Mountain
Mist®. The quilting was done with
cotton thread.

27" x 27"   **Made by Josephine Thogode**

Folk
Dance

For this gentle quilt, Jo chose the
Folk Dance quilting pattern on pages
58-59. For the trapunto batt, she
used a Simplicity polyester batt from
Air-Lite Synthetics, and used Warm
and Natural for the overall batt. The
quilting was done with cotton thread.

Solitude

62" x 62"   Made by Ramona Hilton

Ramona Hilton chose the Quiet Tree
quilting pattern, on page 70, for this,
her first quilt. She used a high-loft
polyester batt for her trapunto batt
and Cotton Classic from Fairfield for
the final batt. Ramona quilted with
cotton thread.

23" x 26"   **Made by Hari Walner**

Good Will to All Swans

Detail shown on cover. This quilt uses the Swanee pattern on page 56, (reduced on a copier to 90% of the size shown in the book). The letters were drawn too small to be easily readable. If you decide to trapunto and quilt lettering on your quilt, keep in mind that the letters will lose definition in the quilting. Make them large enough to show up clearly.

Two layers of Mountain Mist Fatt Batt were used for the trapunto batt and Cotton Classic by Fairfield was used for the final batt.

Loving Hearts

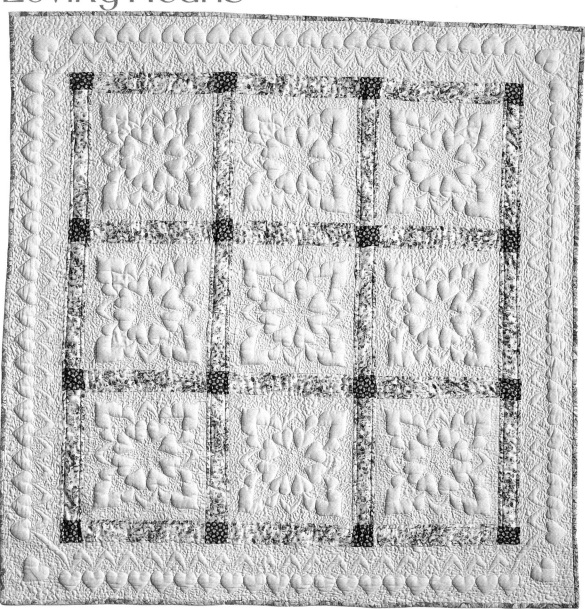

38" x 38"   Made by Maureen Newman

Maureen Newman used the Starry-Eyed block and border patterns on page 66-67 for this wall quilt. For the trapunto batt she used two layers of Fairfield's Ultra Loft and for her final batt she used Heirloom Cotton by Hobbs. The quilting was done with cotton thread.

40" x 40" Made by Linda Graham

Pacific Rose

Linda selected the large rose from Susan B. Anthony, pattern on page 68, and the small rose from the Baby Rose pattern on page 42 for the trapunto/quilting design. She tinted the roses with blusher (from her cosmetic drawer) and the leaves with green pastel chalk, using a cotton swab to blend the colors.

The trapunto batt is a very high-loft polyester and the final batt is Cotton Choice by Mountain Mist.

Homage To
a Watering Can

Danita modified, then trapuntoed,
the Quiet Tree pattern, on page 70,
eliminating the flowers and adding
leaves. Echo quilting surrounds the
motifs. The trapunto batt is a high-
loft polyester and the final batt is
Cotton Choice by Mountain Mist.

42" x 42"   **Made by Danita Rafalovich**

38" x 38"   ***Made by Lynette Fulton***

Teacher's Stuff

This quilt was made by Lynette Fulton, as a teaching aid, to show her students the various effects that different batts give with this machine trapunto technique. The top left square has not been trapuntoed, only quilted. (Lynette says, "I doubt I will ever make a quilt like this again since learning this machine trapunto technique.")

The top right square was trapuntoed using Fairfield's Low-Loft polyester batt, and has only minimal effect. The bottom right square was trapuntoed with Fairfield's Extra Loft® polyester batt and gives more of a stuffed look than the Low-Loft. The bottom left square was trapuntoed with Fairfield's Hi-Loft and gives the most raised effect.

The piecing pattern Lynette used was from *Patched Works* by Trudie Hughes, and the quilting pattern is Simple Manners, shown on page 63.

11" x 23"   *Made by Margie Evans*

Let's Play

"I want to sit under this trapuntoed tree and dream of my next quilt and eat chocolate cake."
—Margie Evans.

The tree is the Cottonwood quilting pattern, given on page 38-39. Mountain Mist's Fatt Batt was used for the trapunto.

Spring Quintet Trapunto

56" x 56"   ***Made by Cheryl Phillips***

Cheryl Phillips used the shadow trapunto technique from Lesson 6 with the Spring Quintet design, on page 54. She used a sheer bastite over a watercolor print fabric for the center of the quilt with the shadow effect.

She used Heirloom Cotton by Hobbs for the trapunto technique as well as for the final batt. The thread Cheryl used for quilting was a pastel variegated rayon thread.

Trout Almond Dean

21" x 14"   Made by Hank Osborn

This environmentally-friendly wall trophy is Hank's first completed quilt. The trapunto batt is a 10 ounce polyester batt by Air-Lite Synthetics and the overall batt is Cotton Choice by Mountain Mist. The quilting design is Over the Rainbow on page 62. Cotton thread was used for quilting.

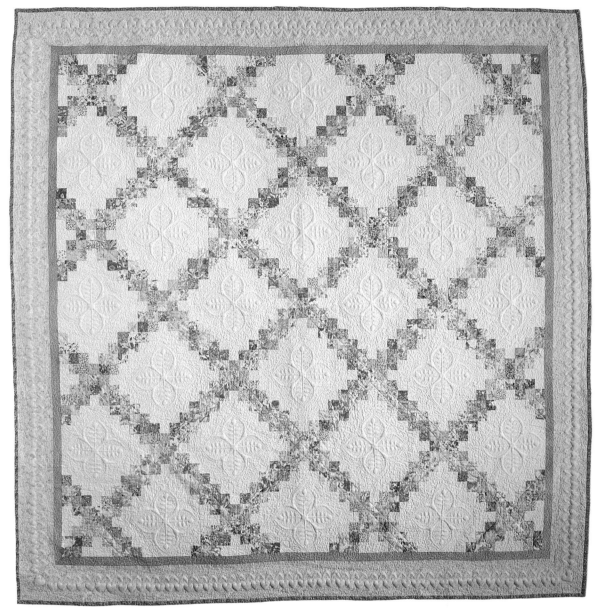

94" x 94"   **Made by Margie Evans**

Ground Hog Day Quilt

The quilting design stitched in the blocks is Autumn's Treasure, found on page 72, and the border design is the Starry-Eyed border, pattern found on page 67. For the trapunto batt, Margie used Fatt Batt by Mountain Mist and for the final batt she used Cotton Choice by Mountain Mist. For quilting and stippling she used rayon thread.

43" x 43"   **Made by Hari Walner**

The Sun is Always Rising

The Swanee pattern on page 56 (enlarged on a copier at 110%) was used as the center quilting motif and the heart segments from Swanee were modified for the border design. The trapunto batt was two layers of Simplicity's polyester Bond Tight, by Air-Lite Synthetics, and the final batt was Cotton Choice by Mountain Mist.

Are We Having Any Fun?

An important aspect of quilting is that it be fun. Relax and enjoy yourself. If you enjoy what you do, you will do more of it. If you do more of it, you will get better at it. If you get better at it, you will enjoy doing it more — a beautiful circle.

Machine quilting, especially for beginners, can be a tension-riddled experience because it demands your complete, undivided attention. Take a few moments to prepare yourself for a good time at your machine. Put your mind and body in a relaxed state. You will learn faster, quilt better, and avoid unwarranted fatigue.

Loosen your body with some simple shoulder rolls and stretch your neck toward each shoulder. Always move slowly and let your body and mind relax. Repeat until you are smiling.

Put on some soft music that you like and have a cup of soothing tea or a glass of milk.

Visualize stitching your designs. Picture yourself calmly and smoothly guiding your quilt, front to back, back to front, and side to side in your friendly machine. Let your mind see the stitched design appearing under the needle — imagine it is every bit as beautiful as you want it to be. If we believe we can accomplish things, we can. You can do wonderful things with a little time and strong belief.

Warm up your stitching arms and eyes for the day by stitching on a scrap sandwich. Find out what your rhythm for the day is before you start quilting.

Quilt only for an hour or two at a time. If you are still having a good time, have another glass of milk, do a few more shoulder rolls, and continue. If you are tiring, do something else. The one who dies with the most quilts made does not win.

If you are new to machine quilting and have a frustrating experience, don't think about your uneven stitches or the lines you missed stitching. Give yourself a hug for all the things you did learn, and apply them the next time.

The memory of making the quilt should be as wonderful as the praises you receive, and deserve, once the quilt is finished. Think of each step of your quiltmaking as the most fun you can have that day. Now, take a deep breath, roll those shoulders, sip that tea, quilt for two hours, hoist that handbag, and go look at more new fabric. Another beautiful circle.

The Quilters

These talented quilters, with their broad range of experience, were asked to make a quilt (or quilts, if they liked) using the techniques and designs from the book. I greatly appreciate their contributions—not only for making these quilts, but also offering good suggestions about the techniques.

Sue Danielson, Golden, Colorado

Sue's busy schedule includes volunteer work for the Rocky Mountain Quilt Museum, active membership in two quilt guilds, and a career as a molecular biologist. Her sense of grace, beauty and tradition, coupled with her excellent machine quilting skills created *Feathered Friend II,* shown on page 24.

Lynette Fulton, Ontario, California

Lynette works as a recovery room nurse to support her quilting habit. She is also a much sought-after teacher of machine quilting, and her bubbly excitement for introducing new techniques to her students overflows. Her two quilts, *Judy's Star* and *Teacher's Stuff,* are shown on pages 50 and 85.

Ramona Hilton, Westminster, Colorado

Ramona loves all the needle arts and has sewn for many years, but has just recently taken up quilting. Her love of family, friends and home is reflected in the warm, comforting colors she likes to work with. Her first quilt, *Solitude,* is on page 80.

Margie Evans, Valencia, California

Margie has been quilting for nine years, and her home is filled with quilts that demonstrate her wonderful sense of fun and adventure. Margie, with husband John, founded Me Sew, Inc., a company that manufactures light tables for quilters. Margie sewed three quilts for this book, *Groundhog Day Quilt, Let's Play* and *Mama's Songbird.* They are shown on pages 89, 86 and 52.

Linda Graham, Los Angeles, California

The phrase, enthusiastic quilter, was coined for stitchers like Linda. Her quilts always have a "Linda" touch and each one reflects another facet of her personality. She is an active member of the Scrappy Quilters Guild in Los Angeles. Her quilt, *Pacific Rose,* is on page 83.

Judy Morin, Hendersonville, North Carolina

The owner of a mail order thread business, The Thread Shed, Judy is always busy checking out new materials and tools, and trying new techniques. Along with this, she has also managed to make wedding quilts for her grown children. How wonderful that she took the time to make *Traditional Chintz Quilt without the Traditional Work,* shown on page 51.

Maureen Newman, Denver, Colorado

After Maureen's first quilt class in 1991, she went home and dug out the sewing machine (given to her 30 years before) from under the house, cleaned it, oiled it, learned how to use it, and zoomed into quiltmaking. She loves to travel and absorbs inspiration from everywhere. Her quilt, *Loving Hearts,* is on page 82.

Hank Osborn, Westminster, Colorado

The year after Hank finished at the University of Iowa, he saw a quilt that inspired him to make one just like it, only larger. While making his king-size quilt, he took time out to make the wall quilt, *Trout Almond Dean* on page 88, which is his first completed quilt.

Danita Rafalovich, Los Angeles, California

Danita is an experienced quilter, teacher, and co-author of *Backart, On the Flipside.* Danita has a degree in Botany and a considerable collection of plants. Her design sense and machine quilting skills are exquisite, as her *Homage to A Watering Can,* on page 84 shows.

Shirley Wegert, Englewood, Colorado

Although Shirley has made dozens upon dozens of hand quilted quilts, she is now also machine quilting. She is not only a very active member in The Arapahoe County Quilters and the Colorado Quilting Council, but she is also an avid cyclist. Her superb piecing skills are a marvel in the Denver area. Shirley pieced *Irish Tenors* on page 25.

Cheryl Osborn, Westminster, Colorado

Cheryl has always liked handwork, but is new to using the sewing machine. She is a life-long teacher of another art form, baton twirling. She jumped right in when asked to study the techniques and make a quilt for the book. *Fantastic Beginning,* her first quilt (page 23), was done entirely on the machine.

Cheryl Phillips, Fruita, Colorado

Cheryl's unbelievable artistic energy and belief in the creativity within everyone has made her a very popular machine quilting teacher. She is a great experimenter and fearless in trying new techniques. She authored *Quilts Without Corners.* The quilt she made for this book, *Spring Quintet Trapunto,* is shown on page 87.

Josephine Thogode, Denver, Colorado

Jo retired from her career as a grade-school librarian, but she certainly did not retire from sewing. After years of making crafts and sewing dolls and bears, Josephine discovered the world of quilting in 1993. Her excitement and skills grow with each new project. Her quilt, *Folk Dance,* is on page 79.

Bibliography

Heirloom Machine Quilting, Revised 3rd edition,
Harriet Hargrave, 1995,
C&T Publishing

(excellent source for batting information)

The Complete Book of Machine Quilting, 2nd edition,
Robbie and Tony Fanning, 1994,
Chilton Book Company

Teach Yourself Machine Piecing and Quilting,
Debra Wagner, 1992,
Chilton Book Company

Quilts and Quilting from Threads, 1991,
The Taunton Press, Inc.

Fun and Fancy Machine Quiltmaking,
Lois Tornquist Smith, 1989,
American Quilter's Society

Quilting by Machine,
Singer Reference Library, 1990,
Cy DeCross Incorporated

Sources

Air-Lite Synthetics
Manufacturing
Simplicity Bond Tight
10 oz. polyester batt
342 Irwin Street
Pontiac, MI 48341-2982

Beautiful Publications, LLC
ContinuousLine
quilting patterns
13340 Harrison Street
Thornton, CO 80241-1403

Cherrywood Fabrics, Inc.
hand-dyed fabrics
P.O.Box 486
Brainerd, MN 56401-0486

Fairfield Processing Corp.
Poly-fil Cotton Classic,
Hi-Loft, Ultra-Loft, Extra-Loft
P.O. Box 1130MJ
Danbury, CT 06813-1130

Fiskars
scissors and sewing supplies
7811 West Stewart Avenue
Wausau, WI 54401

Hobbs Bonded Fibers
Heirloom Cotton batting
P.O. Box 3000
Mexia, TX 76667

Little Foot Inc.
Big Foot free-motion
darning foot
605 Bledsoe N.W.
Albuquerque, NM 87107

Me Sew, Inc.
light tables
24307 Magic Mountain
Parkway, #195
Valencia, CA 91355

Pfaff American Sales Corp.
Pfaff 7550 sewing machine
610 Winters Avenue
Paramus, NJ 07653

Robert Kaufman Fabrics
100% cotton Ultra Sateen
129 W. 132nd Street
Los Angeles, CA 90059

Stearns Technical Textiles
Mountain Mist Cotton Choice
Mountain Mist Fatt Batt
100 Williams Street
Cincinnati, OH 45215

Viking Husquevarna
Viking Husquevarna #1
sewing machines
11760 Berea Road
Cleveland, OH 44111

Warm Products, Inc.
Warm & Natural batting
16110 Woodinville-Redmond Rd.
Woodinville, WA 98072

YLI Corporation
distributors of Wash-Away
thread
P.O. Box 109
Provo, UT 84603-0109

Other Fine Books From C&T Publishing

Appliqué 12 Easy Ways! : Charming Quilts, Giftable Projects & Timeless Techniques,
Elly Sienkiewicz

The Art of Classic Quiltmaking,
Harriet Hargrave and
Sharyn Craig

At Home with Patrick Lose: Colorful Quilted Projects,
Patrick Lose

Color From the Heart: Seven Great Ways to Make Quilts with Colors You Love,
Gai Perry

Curves in Motion: Quilt Designs & Techniques,
Judy B. Dales

Fabric Shopping with Alex Anderson, Seven Project to Help You: Make, Successful Choices, Build Your Confidence, Add to Your Fabric Stash,
Alex Anderson

Fantastic Fabric Folding: Innovative Quilting Projects,
Rebecca Wat

Freddy's House: Brilliant Color in Quilts,
Freddy Moran

Free Stuff for Collectors on the Internet,
Judy Heim and Gloria Hansen

Free Stuff for Crafty Kids on the Internet,
Judy Heim and Gloria Hansen

Free Stuff for Gardeners on the Internet,
Judy Heim and Gloria Hansen

Free Stuff for Quilters on the Internet, 2nd Ed.,
Judy Heim and Gloria Hansen

Free Stuff for Sewing Fanatics on the Internet,
Judy Heim and Gloria Hansen

Free Stuff for Stitchers on the Internet,
Judy Heim and Gloria Hansen

Heirloom Machine Quilting, Third Edition,
Harriet Hargrave

Make Any Block Any Size,
Joen Wolfrom

Mastering Quilt Marking: Marking Tools & Techniques, Choosing Stencils, Matching Borders & Corners,
Pepper Cory

The New England Quilt Museum Quilts: Featuring the Story of the Mill Girls. With Instructions for 5 Heirloom Quilts,
Jennifer Gilbert

The Photo Transfer Handbook: Snap It, Print It, Stitch It!,
Jean Ray Laury

Pieced Flowers,
Ruth B. McDowell

Pieced Roman Shades: Turn Your Favorite Quilt Patterns into Window Hangings,
Terrell Sundermann

Piecing: Expanding the Basics,
Ruth B. McDowell

Quilt It for Kids; 11 Projects, Sports, Fantasy & Animal Themes, Quilts for Children of All Ages,
Pam Bono

Quilts from Europe, Projects and Inspiration,
Gül Laporte

Rotary Cutting with Alex Anderson: Tips, Techniques, and Projects,
Alex Anderson

Rx for Quilters: Stitcher-Friendly Advice for Every Body,
Susan Delaney Mech, M.D.

Shadow Quilts: Easy to Design Multiple Image Quilts,
Patricia Magaret and
Donna Slusser

Skydyes: A Visual Guide to Fabric Painting,
Mickey Lawler

Small Scale Quiltmaking: Precision, Proportion, and Detail,
Sally Collins

Special Delivery Quilts,
Patrick Lose

Start Quilting with Alex Anderson: Six Projects for First-Time Quilters,
Alex Anderson

Through the Garden Gate: Quilters and Their Gardens,
Jean and Valori Wells

Trapunto by Machine,
Hari Walner

Travels with Peaky and Spike: Doreen Speckmann's Quilting Adventures,
Doreen Speckmann

Wild Birds: Designs for Appliqué & Quilting,
Carol Armstrong

Wildflowers: Designs for Appliqué & Quilting,
Carol Armstrong

Women of Taste: A Collaboration Celebrating Quilt Artists and Chefs,
Girls, Inc.

For more information write for a free catalog:

C&T Publishing, Inc.
P.O. Box 1456
Lafayette, CA 94549
(800) 284-1114
web: www.ctpub.com
e-mail: ctinfo@ctpub.com

For quilting supplies:
Cotton Patch Mail Order
3405 Hall Lane, Dept. CTB
Lafayette, CA 94549
web: www.quiltusa.com
e-mail: quiltusa@yahoo.com
(800) 835-4418
(925) 283-7883

About the Author

With a background in illustration, and teaching painting and drawing, Hari Walner began designing and making quilts in 1987 when she was hired by Leman Publications as an illustrator for their quilt magazines. She immediately began making quilts and decided that the tight definition of lines that machine quilting offered was much like drawing, a skill she has always enjoyed. She also found that machine quilting was easier when you could quilt in long, unbroken lines, so she co-founded with Gordon Snow, Beautiful Publications, a publishing house specializing in continuous-line quilting designs.

When their business began exhibiting at trade and consumer shows for quilters, Hari began to demonstrate and teach machine quilting.

Ever experimenting, reading, trying new techniques and testing new ideas, she is grateful to all the quilters, students and writers who have taught her so much. This book is a result of some of that learning and experimenting.

Hari lives in Colorado with her partner/husband, Gordon. They share and love three adult children and three grandchildren.